THE
CHALLENGES
OF ISRAEL

THE CHALLENGES OF ISRAEL

by

Ora Shem-Ur

SHENGOLD PUBLISHERS, INC.
New York

ISBN 0-88400-071-0
Library of Congress Catalog Card Number: 80-52915
Copyright © 1980 by Ora Shem-Ur
Published by Shengold Publishers, Inc.
New York, N.Y. 10036
Printed in the United States of America

CONTENTS

1. The World and Israel 7
2. Flashback 8
3. There Are Neither Palestinians Nor Jordanians 11
4. Peace and War 15
5. Demography 21
6. The Jews Are Coming 30
7. The Zionists Are Coming 32
8. Arab Nationalism 36
9. The Arabists 38
10. The Establishment of Israel 43
11. Israel and the Arab World 47
12. Confrontation 52
13. A Question of Survival 58
14. The Territorial Imperative 64
15. Secure Frontiers 72
16. Israel Dominates the Middle East 75
Map 9
Demographical Table 1 24
Demographical Table 2 28
Graphs 67

FOREWORD

My aim in writing this book is to analyze the crucial issues facing Israel. These problems of war or peace with the Arabs, conceding the territories, settlements and demography, involve the whole world.

I will examine the existing facts objectively, without illusions or wishful thinking. By probing Middle East tensions, I hope to reach a correct diagnosis which offers relevant conclusions concerning the welfare of my country and people. These findings must of necessity include ways of:

Assuring the continued existence and sovereignty of the State of Israel.

Guaranteeing the prosperity and growth of Israel, and the safeguarding of its Jewish character.

Supporting fulfillment of the age-old aspiration of the Jewish people: The return to Zion.

Contrary to the customary Zionist literature, I do not rely on the right of the Jewish people to the Land of Israel, be it religious or historic. Neither do I concern myself with any ideology: Zionist, social or humanitarian. In my analysis, I only consider the current situation: Israel has a Jewish population of about three million which is growing steadily. Israel holds the Land of Israel which it intends to keep forever. Israel possesses one of the best military forces in the Middle East and is a dominant power.

I wish to point out that my aim in writing this book is to inform. I do not intend to advocate Israel's case. The Jewish nation and the State of Israel are not appearing before any international tribunal, nor do they need the verdict of any such body.

Of course, any community — as does any individual — needs and desires sympathy. If this presentation helps clarify distorted "facts," this book will have served its purpose.

I also wish to point out that the views presented here are my own. Still, as a writer and columnist who is active in Israel's political struggles, I am sure that a large segment of the Israel population feels as I do.

1. THE WORLD AND ISRAEL

The Arab-Israel conflict and tension in the Middle East hold the attention of the entire world.

Presidents, ministers, diplomats, newspapers, radio and television commentators, intellectuals and even the man-in-the-street are preoccupied with this problem. It is almost as if it is the most important crisis on earth, demanding an urgent solution.

The Middle East situation, so it seems, is even more compelling than the starvation of millions in Asia and Africa; more perilous than the population explosion; more dangerous than pollution; and even more serious than the enslavement of peoples under totalitarian regimes.

True, the fact that half of Europe is subjugated by the Communists and that innocent people are hauled off to work camps in Siberia, as well as to mental hospitals, is not very palatable to the Western world.

But to Westerners, even the plight of political and social prisoners is nothing compared to that of the "Palestinians." These are the same Palestinians who in 1948, goaded on by their own leaders, fled from their homes and now live in camps with their coreligionists in the nation states of the great Arab homeland which overflows with oil and petro-dollars.

These "refugees" must be saved, say world leaders. They must be helped. Their problem is the most "burning question" of enlightened people. It seems that as long as the Palestinian issue is not solved, the progressive conscience of humanity will not find peace of mind! The West apparently has a selective conscience. It prefers to ignore the existence of others, such as those fleeing from Vietnam, Cambodia, India, Pakistan, Bangladesh, Cyprus and Lebanon.

Millions of refugees exist in the world. Most of them have

adjusted to their new locales where they began anew, with or without help. But only the Palestinians are kept by their own brothers for over thirty years as "refugees" in camps. Used as a political weapon against Israel, these Palestinians are prevented from rehabilitating themselves and integrating into their new lands.

Many nations and groups meddle in the Middle East. Each, according to its own vested interest, introduces its formula for a solution to the area's problem.

But there is a consensus in the West, as well as in the East, that Israel must hand over the territories now under its administration to the Arabs. The problem is that what they call Arab-occupied territories are actually part of the national heritage of the Jewish people: The Land of Israel.

2. FLASHBACK

The Arab-Israel conflict is one of the most controversial topics in the world today. But in spite of the interest in the issue, few analysts have made their way down to the very roots and true motivations of the strife that exists between Israel and the Arab world. Governments, statesmen and even the media frequently base their policies on incorrect and unrealistic assumptions.

The truth is that except for the experts, few have any real knowledge of the area's geography. Fewer still can evaluate correctly the geopolitical importance of the West Bank, Judea and Samaria, the Golan Heights or the Sinai Peninsula.

It is crucial to be able to understand Middle East geography. The State of Israel is located on the eastern shore of the Mediterranean. Israel itself is bordered on the south by the Gulf of Eilat and the Red Sea. But modern Israel is only a part of the vast area that once was the Syrian Province of the Ottoman Empire of Turkey. Until it was conquered by the British in 1917, this whole province was one integral unit. It extended from the borders of Turkey in the north to the Suez Canal in the south. At that time, the Suez Canal was the international border with Egypt. Included in this area was the land that now makes up the states of Jordan and Israel. The administrative center of this

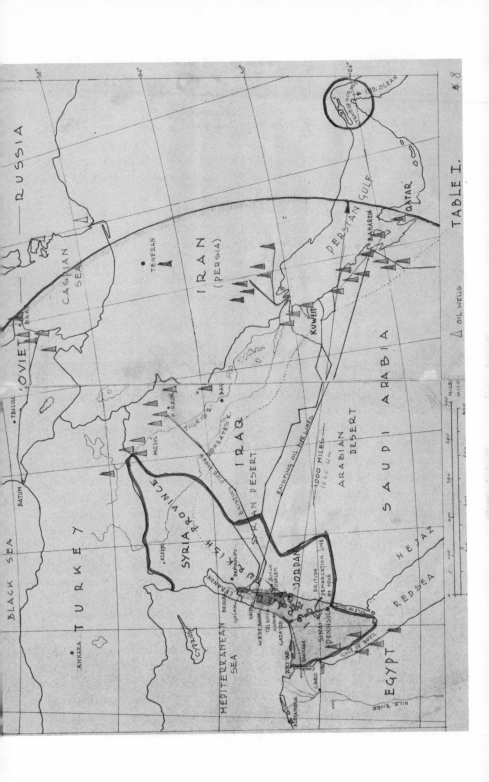

TABLE I.

△ OIL WELLS

geographical entity was the city of Damascus where the Turkish Governor maintained his headquarters.

The Sinai Peninsula also was part of this Turkish province. But in 1906, Turkey was forced to cede the administration of the Sinai to the British. The latter were interested in removing the Turks from the Suez Canal Zone. In the Map the broken line between a point south of Gaza on the Mediterranean and running southeast to the Gulf of Eilat marks the boundary of the former British administrative area of Sinai. Yet the international border between Turkey and Egypt ran along the Suez Canal and remained unchanged. Indeed, until the expiration of the British Mandate in 1948, passport and customs checks were carried out at the train station of Kantara located on the banks of the Suez.

During the 30 years of the British Mandate, a British District Officer was in charge of the Sinai Peninsula. This officer served under the British High Commissioner located in Jerusalem and was not under the Commissioner in Cairo. The officer's job was to supervise thousands of Arab nomads who inhabited the Sinai oasis. The Egyptians are neither of Arabic descent, nor are they nomads.

Except in ancient times when they engaged in copper mining, the Egyptians have never lived in the Sinai Desert.

Therefore, the Egyptian claim that the Sinai is "Egyptian soil" has no national, ethnic or political grounds whatsoever.

Eighty-five per cent of the former Turkish Province of Syria is desert, including the Syrian Desert, the Arabian Desert, the Negev, and the Sinai. The dotted line contains the least yearly rainfall, i.e. it serves as the border line between the desert and the rich area of the Fertile Crescent.

The southern part of the Turkish Province includes the present states of Israel and Jordan. This area, known formerly as Palestine, was the most miserable, poverty-stricken and under-populated region in all of the Ottoman Empire. Indeed, it is estimated that one hundred years ago, Palestine, which included the area on both banks of the Jordan, was populated by no more than 200,000 inhabitants, including 40,000 Jews. It was this area which was resettled by Jews. And it was a century ago that they returned to their Land of Israel. In 1878, the first Jewish "colony," Petach Tikva (The Gate of Hope), was established. Today, Petach Tikva is a town of 100,000.

Two famous American travellers testified to the situation in the Holy Land at that time. Both were shocked by the terrible neglect.

In 1857 Herman Melville wrote in the *Travel Journal:*

". . . whitish mildew pervading whole tracts of landscape — bleached — leprosy encrustation of curses — old cheese — bones of rock — crunched, gnawed and mumbled — mere refuse and rubbish of creation — like that laying outside the Jaffa Gate — all Judea seems to have been accumulations of this rubbish — No moss as in other ruins — no ivy — the unleavening nakedness of desolation — no grace of decay — whitish ashes — lime-kilns . . . Village of Lepers — houses facing the wall — Zion. Their park, a dung-heap. They sit by the gates asking alms — then whine — avoidance of them and horror . . ."

In 1869, Mark Twain wrote:

". . . Palestine sits in sackcloth and ashes. Over it broods the spell of a curse that has withered its fields and fettered its energies . . . Nazareth is forlorn; about that ford of Jordan where the hosts of Israel entered the Promised Land with songs of rejoicing, one finds only a squalid camp of fantastic Bedouins . . . Palestine is desolate and unlovely . . ."

3. THERE ARE NEITHER PALESTINIANS NOR JORDANIANS

While the population of the Syrian Turkish Province which stretched from Turkey to the Suez Canal was a single geographical unit, the population itself was composed of three distinct elements: urban residents, farmers and Bedouins.

Most of the urban populace consisted of Arab-speaking Moslems. They were merchants and craftsmen. Educated clerks, teachers, clerics and landowners made up a small group. In addition, there were several minority groups, such as, Arab Christians, Armenians, Greeks and a few Europeans and Jews.

11

The cultural and ethnic composition of the urban dwellers — including language and customs — was the same in all the cities of the Middle East. From Aleppo in the north to Damascus, Jerusalem and Jaffa in the south, there was a common civilization. In the West, it was given the name "The Levantine Society." Indeed, the people themselves were called Levantine.

In Lebanon, Beirut served as a center for the larger Christian and Maronite minorities who lived mostly in the towns and villages. Here, too, their language and customs were Arabic, though they did assimilate some Western influences, especially those of the French. But all of them, Christian and Moslem, saw themselves as members of a single people: the Arabs.

The great majority of the *fellahin* in this area were Arab-speaking Moslems. Apart from a few minority villages, these rural inhabitants of the former Turkish Province consisted of one homogeneous ethnic entity. They spoke the same language. They possessed the same customs, religion and moral values. They ate the same food. They tilled their land by using methods of extensive agriculture, depending, of course, on the amount of yearly rainfall in their region.

The *fellahin* in the area are organized into large family units, the hamulas. In each village, there are a number of these hamulas which are ruled by the elders. Often, opposing families would engage in a blood feud that would last for generations.

All the fellahin in the former Turkish-Syrian Province consider themselves Arabs. On the other hand, the fellahin of Egypt, who also speak Arabic, consider themselves, Egyptians.

The third element in the area is the nomadic tribes of sheep herders and tent dwellers. They, too, are Arab-speaking Moslems. They roam the area and seek grazing spots. They put up their tents. They graze their sheep. After this, they move on. They have no fixed home. Their encampments covered vast areas, from northern Syria to Iraq and down to Saudi Arabia. On the other hand, each tribe once claimed a specific piece of land, to which they would return from time to time.

The Bedouins consider themselves true Arabs, descendants of the tribes who first recognized Mohammed as their prophet.

They stick to their old ways. They still prefer their tents. To force them to become house dwellers takes a great deal of persuasion.

These then are the three elements that make up the population of the former Turkish Province of Syria. All of them were Turkish citizens. But their nationality was Syrian Arab.

During the centuries of Turkish rule, these Arabs had no political identity. They did not have any aspirations for self-determination, nor for a break from the Ottoman Empire, as was the case of Egypt.

The new Arab states did not come into existence until after World War I and after the disintegration of the Ottoman Empire. They were not created as a result of Arab desire for independence. The victorious British and French partitioned the area among themselves. In the north, two states, Syria and Lebanon, were established under a French Mandate. Great Britain was given the mandate for the south by the League of Nations. Britain became the protectorate over a land mass that extended to the land on both banks of the Jordan. The British gave this area the ancient Roman name of Palestine.

It should be remembered that the Powers partitioned the area not according to ethnic or national criteria as, for example, was done in the Balkans. There, one could clearly define the borders that existed between Czechs and Austrians; between Greeks, Yugoslavs and Bulgarians. These units contained homogeneous peoples and their claims for self-determination were justified. But the Syrian Province of the former Ottoman Empire was not divided according to ethnic entities — because there simply were no ethnic differences.

The Syrian Turkish Province was occupied by only one people: the Syrian Arabs. There is no difference between an Arab of Damascus and an Arab of Jerusalem.

The claim that there is a so-called "Palestinian nation" is ridiculous and groundless. There is no Palestinian nation, nor is there a "Palestinian entity." Moreover, there never has been a Jordanian nation.

The nation of Jordan was created in 1922. Its midwife was the British Colonial Secretary, Winston S. Churchill. In one fell swoop, Mr. Churchill gave away more than

two-thirds of the area of Palestine that had been placed under the British Mandate by the League of Nations for a Jewish National Home. His creation of a separate English protectorate called "Jordan," was contrary to the promises the British gave to the Jews, as well as a betrayal of the Articles of the Mandate.

The only function of this desert state, Jordan, has been to serve as an imperialistic base to safeguard British interests in the area, especially oil interests of the "Iraq Petroleum Oil Company" (IPC) whose pipelines stretched from Kirkuk to Haifa. To defend the pipeline, the British created the Arab Legion consisting mostly of Bedouins commanded by British officers. As head of this new protectorate, the British nominated as their puppet, an Arab Chieftain, the Emir Abdullah ibn Hussein from Hejaz, King Hussein's grandfather.

The fact that this area was governed by a separate administration and that its name was changed to Jordan did not turn its Syrian-Arab inhabitants into a "Jordanian nation."

Even today, the Hashemite Kingdom of Jordan remains an imperialistic base and, as it was under the British, it has no viable means to sustain economic or political independence.

The renaissance of the "Palestinian nation" is very recent. This "nation" was created just thirteen years ago.

After the Six-Day War of 1967, the Jordanian West Bank came under Israeli rule. Prior to the war, the Arab inhabitants of the West Bank considered themselves "Jordanians." Even today, they hold Jordanian passports. But now they declare that they are a "Palestinian people." At the same time, the inhabitants of the Gaza Strip who considered themselves to be Egyptians before 1967, now also declare themselves to be "Palestinian."

But the "Palestinian nation" is nothing but an invention of the Arab states who use it as a lever to oust the Jews from the "Arab Middle East."

a piece of cheese in its beak. Wishing to get the cheese, the fox employs every ploy and use of flattery he knows — and succeeds.

In our opinion, all these suggestions are worthless. We shall not be tempted.

But, hypothetically, let us suppose that we are willing to consider security guarantees that are offered to us. We remember that after the 1956 Sinai Campaign, the U.S., Britain and France gave Israel guarantees for free shipping in the Straits of Tiran in exchange for Israel surrendering occupied Sinai to Egypt.

However, in 1967, the Egyptians again closed the Straits of Tiran. They blocked our shipping to Africa and the Far East. Despite our entreaties, our guarantors did not intervene, nor did they react.

Let us carry the argument further. This time, let us assume that we gave up the territories and that our guarantors sincerely wished to come to our aid if we are attacked by the Arabs. But, considering the lightning speed of modern warfare, their help is bound to come too late.

While the guarantors convene, argue, affirm and finally decide to send military aid, tens of thousands of Israelis will be dead; Israel will be occupied.

We do not have to go far to find a concrete example that if we agree to exchange secure borders for guarantees by foreign powers, we face destruction. Is it almost forgotten that not long ago, the Turks invaded our neighbor Cyprus. In a few days, thousands of Greek Cypriots were massacred and two hundred thousand became penniless refugees.

Another example is Lebanon. Despite the fact that France and the U.S. are considered the traditional protectors of Lebanese Christians, and despite the fact that the whole world was genuinely shocked by the atrocities committed in that country, nobody really gave up "their morning cup of coffee and newspaper," newspapers which carried eyewitness accounts of the killing, destruction, cruelty, massacres and terrible sufferings of tens of thousands of Lebanese. This northern neighbor of Israel was almost completely destroyed. The world looked the other way. That world is Christian. The victims are Christian. How can we who are Jews count on guarantees and promises by a Christian world that is oblivious to the plight of its own co-religionists?

To me it is quite clear that were Israel and the Israelis

destroyed, no one would deviate "one iota" from his daily routine. I do not blame anybody. I probably would act the same way if one of the Western countries which I enjoy visiting would be destroyed.

The one — and only one — conclusion that we Israelis can draw from the above examples, is that Israel can not count on any guarantees, or promises by guarantors, whoever they are. To survive, we have to keep the enemy as far away as possible from our cities and settlements. We have to maintain wide defensive perimeters that will make it possible to contain future aggression.

But when the persuasion and friendly pressures do not work and Israel does not give in, our so-called well-wishers switch to veiled threats. In the beginning, they were voiced by Dr. Henry Kissinger. Now they are expressed by Prof. Zbigniew Brzezinski, who employs scare tactics. They tell us the alternative is war and disaster. Unless you withdraw, they say, the Arabs will wage another war and there will be more casualties. And that is not all. You can be sure, they continue, the Arabs again will place an embargo on oil shipments. Then the economy of Europe, Japan and the U.S. will collapse. A global war might break out and it will be more destructive than ever. And all because of the obstinacy of the Jews.

Using these arguments, the Western governments cynically demand that Israel sacrifice her national interests and security for the sake of the U.S., Japan and other Western nations.

But Israel refuses to be the offering on the altar of these or other foreign interests.

Let me also reply to the threats of the Arabs and their supporters that our "obstinacy" will bring down upon us a total and destructive war and that the number of killed in the next conflagration will be unprecedented.

My answer is that from the first day of Israel's independence in 1948, the Arab states have waged four wars against Israel in order to annihilate the new state. They always have possessed overwhelming superiority, both in manpower and material. But, they were decisively beaten on four occasions.

Tens of thousands of their soldiers were taken prisoners. Their war material was destroyed. They lost land. In all four aggressive acts against Israel, the Arabs have been saved at the crucial moment of total collapse by armistices that had been imposed on Israel by brutal Soviet threats and heavy American pressure.

In the War of 1973, Israel was taken by surprise on her most holy of Holy Days, Yom Kippur. Because of erroneous evaluations by Israeli intelligence, the vast majority of our Army personnel was on leave. Transportation was at a standstill. Aided by meticulous preparation and Russian advice, the Egyptian and Syrian armies attacked at the same time. Thousands of tanks, hundreds of fighter planes and over a million men comprised the force of the aggressors.

This vast invading army, the size of which was only reached previously in the World War II Battle of Stalingrad, immediately overran the Israeli lines. On the southern front, the Egyptians crossed the Suez Canal and deployed their forces all along the eastern (Israeli) side of the Canal. On the northern front the Syrians swept through the Golan Heights and reached the former Israeli borders. An Arab victory seemed close at hand.

In the midst of this seemingly hopeless situation, Israel's reserve forces began to organize. They stopped the enemy and counterattacked. In ten days, Israel's Defense Forces drove the Syrians back out of the Golan Heights. In fact, Israel moved to within 26 miles of Damascus.

In a brilliant operation devised by General Ariel Sharon, the I.D.F. cut the Egyptian Army in two on the southern front and crossed the Suez Canal. It took the I.D.F. only six more days to advance to the approaches of the cities of Ismailia and Suez. The Israelis were only 62 miles from Cairo. Starting the war at a disadvantage and having been taken by surprise, Israel won one of the most brilliant victories in military history in sixteen days.

Again, as in the previous wars, the total collapse of the Arab armies had been prevented because of the intervention of the U.S. Dr. Kissinger's manipulations; his pressures and threats; and his promises of billions of dollars in long-term aid on the one hand, as well as a genuine hope of peace on the other hand, broke the resistance of Israeli leaders. Israel was again robbed of the fruits of its victory.

It is clear that we missed the opportunity of forcing the enemy to sign a comprehensive peace treaty, and so we bared ourselves to renewed threats and more wars. What has been done can not be undone. We can, however, learn from our mistakes and draw the proper conclusions.

Israel's military leaders and foreign military experts believe that the I.D.F. is still, and I underline the word, "still," the most powerful army in the area, capable of defeating all the combined Arab armies.

One can assume, therefore, that if Arab fanaticism and intransigence force us into another war, we will not repeat our previous mistake. We will not let anyone again rob us of a decisive victory.

Moreover, we must also remember that in the Yom Kippur War, a war that was waged far from our towns and settlements, we suffered 3,000 casualties. If we abandon the West Bank and Gaza Strip, it is clear that in future attacks launched against us from across those new borders which are close to our populated areas, we might suffer tens of thousands of casualties, even if we win that war.

It is a cold and cruel, statistical count. But nobody denies its credibility. The odds of our soldiers and civilians staying alive will be far greater if we hold to our present, more secure and distant borders.

Some Israelies ask: "How long shall we have to fight? After years of persecution and oppression, we came to this country to find peace and security . . ."

The answer to this question is not ours. We shall fight as long as we have to defend our land. We shall do it just as have all nations for thousands of years, as long as we are surrounded by aggressive neighbors coveting our land.

In World War II, the Soviet Union sacrificed twenty million men to defend the motherland. The Russians certainly could have "come to terms" with the Germans in exchange for the Ukraine or Byelorussia. They did not. Free people do not barter away pieces of their homeland.

In addition, every Israeli must be aware of the fact that wars occur in all parts of the world, not just in Israel. We are not the only state whose sons are facing dangers. Tens of thousands of Jews — citizens of various countries — have been killed serving in the armies of Russia, Poland, Britain and France. In two

American World Wars, the Korean War and the Vietnam War, American Jews, too, gave up their lives for their country. The world is no paradise. Today's détente can turn overnight into a bloody war.

Jews who live in the Diaspora, as well as those seeking ways to escape the dangers they may face in Israel by emigrating, will not be immune from the dangers of war — anywhere. In addition, the questions that are often asked: "How long shall we have to fight? How many more times shall we have to mourn fallen sons and husbands?" is a legitimate question asked by a mother, a father and a wife. The primary concern of the leaders should be the preservation of the whole nation. Asking the above questions signifies a defeatist attitude which says: "Let us give them what they want. Perhaps then, they will let us live in peace." This is a dangerous attitude and illusion.

The Arabs will never let Israel live in peace. No concessions will satiate their appetite.

5. DEMOGRAPHY

I have presented a general outline of the confrontation between Jews and the Arabs and their supporters. Before continuing with a more detailed analysis of this tension as well as conclusions, I wish to focus on an issue which will be of crucial importance to Israel even after the present conflict will be resolved satisfactorily. This critical issue is demography, namely the high birth rate of the Arab population in Israel.

Most Israelis and their leaders tend to brush this issue under the carpet. So do the official statisticians who limit themselves to a forecast of twenty years only — a period which is non-conclusive.

According to the Government of Israel Statistical Yearbook of 1977 the population of Israel was:

JEWS	ARABS	
3,065,000	In Israel (1967 borders)	670,000
	In the West Bank	700,000
	In the Gaza Strip	430,000
Total 3,065,000	Total	1,700,000

According to the same Yearbook, the yearly birth rate of Jews was about 1.75 per cent and that of the Arabs within the pre-1967 borders around 4 per cent. This Arab birth rate is one of the highest in the world.

These birth rate figures show that the Jewish population doubles every forty years, while that of the Arabs double every twenty. In other words, in forty years, the Jewish population will be doubled and the Arab population will grow four times its present size. This is a stunning and unprecedented progression.

Various factions in Israel are engaged in a heated controversy: Whether to return the "occupied territories" to the Arabs in order to achieve peace.

The Israel Labor Party, the "liberals" and generally all the left-wing groups are in favor of returning some or most of the occupied territories and keeping only those "which are required for our security."

They also argue that the annexation of all territories would increase the Arab minority to 36 per cent of the total population. Such a minority, they maintain, would endanger the Jewish character of Israel. It is somewhat paradoxical that the socialists and leftists whose motto is "brotherhood of nations" should be those who favor ethnic *"apartheid."*

On the other hand, the patriotic center and the right are prepared to live side by side with the Arabs and will not give up any part of the Jewish Homeland, the traditional "Land of Israel," even for peace.

In answer to the argument of the leftists expressing their concern over fear of a Jewish minority, the patriots reply that this deficiency will be balanced by a large Jewish immigration to Israel.

Let us examine the viewpoints of both sides:

First, the argument of the patriots who support annexation of the territories.

In all areas now under Israeli control, i.e., in "Greater Israel," the Arabs today comprise 36 per cent of the total population, 1 Arab for 1.8 Jews.

To hold the same ratio in the future, Jewish immigration

will be needed to make up the difference in the relative birthrate increases of Jews and Arabs.

If we take the average Arab birthrate as being 3.75 per cent and the Jewish birthrate as 1.75 per cent and if we assume a slow decrease of future birthrates, then Table I will indicate the growth of the population of Israel, including the occupied territories.

Column A shows the number of Jews rising from natural increase — without any immigration (aliya).

Column B shows the present number of Jews and assumes an optimal immigration. This indicates that the present Jewish population will double in 20 years to six million. From then on, according to the chart there will be a yearly net immigration of about 20,000 Jews.

Column C shows the number of Arabs rising from natural increase.

In order to keep the 1:1.8 ratio, the number of Jews in 20 years should be, according to Table I: 3.5 million Arabs x 1.8 equals 6.3 million Jews. But by natural increase, it will be only 4.3 million Jews; thus a deficiency of two million.

This deficiency will have to be made up during those years by an average, net immigration of 100,000 per annum (abstracting the ones who return).

If the same ratio of 1:1.8 is to be kept 20 more years, then the number of Jews at the end of 40 years should be: 7.3 million Arabs x 1.8 equaling 13.1 million. But by natural increase, it will only be 8.8 million, thus a deficiency of 4.3 million.

Consequently, in 20 to 40 years, an average net immigration of over 200,000 Jews per annum will be required.

If we continue this analysis another 20 years, we shall find that at the end of 60 years there will be a deficiency of 13.5 million Jews, or a required yearly immigration of 650,000 Jews.

That number is absurd: there simply will not be that many Jews alive in the Diaspora (outside of Israel) let alone whether they would be prepared to emigrate.

This analysis was prepared to show that there is no way whatsoever to maintain the present ratio between Jews and Arabs. Even with the optimal possible immigration (aliya) the percentage of the Arabs in Greater Israel will steadily increase until they become the majority.

The only question is: How long will it take?

1 ,GREATER ISRAEL' INCLUDING ,OCCUPIED TERRITORIES' DEMOGRAPHICAL FORECAST – IN MILLIONS –

A   JEWS, FROM NATURAL INCREASE, WITHOUT, IMMIGRATION
B   JEWS, FROM NATURAL INCREASE AND OPTIMAL IMMIGR.
C   ARABS, FR. NATURAL INCREASE

		A	C		B
	YEARS	JEWS	ARABS		JEWS
	1977	3.07	1.7	35.6% →	3.07
PARITY +30	+ 20	4.3	3.5	36.8%	6.0
± 50	+ 40	6.1	7.3	45.%	8.8
	+ 60	8.4	14.5	54%	12.5
	+ 80	11.6	29		17.4

PARITY

According to Columns A and C of Table 1, we can see that without a significant immigration, the line of parity between Jews and Arabs will be reached in about 30 years.

In the case of an optimal immigration as in Column B, the line of parity will be reached only 20 years later — i.e. 50 years at most.

The meaning of these "lines" is that beyond them, the Jewish majority becomes a minority. It also signifies that in 30 to 50 years from now, the Israelis will lose their supremacy in Greater Israel. Or put another way, the Israelis will lose the Jewish State of Israel without a single shot being fired.

This forecast prima facie shows that the arguments of those who oppose the annexation of the West Bank and the Gaza Strip are justified.

When confronted with this problem, many Israeli patriots who are not conscious of the demographic issues reply that the forecast is not so bad as it looks. They believe that in time the Arabs will learn to adapt themselves to the standards of their Jewish neighbors, and that this process will result in a reduced Arab birthrate until it equals that of the Jews. They add that many young Arabs are leaving the West Bank for the oil fields of Saudi Arabia and Kuwait. But the assumption of the patriots is false.

In the booklet, *Population,* published by the Government Information Center in 1977, Dr. D. dela Pergola of the Demographic Department of the Hebrew University of Jerusalem writes:

". . . if the contact with Israel continues, it is to be expected that the death rate of the population of these areas (Judea, Samaria and the Gaza Strip) will decrease and equal that of the Israeli Arabs, i.e. there will be *a rise* in the birthrate. In the more distant future, there will probably be also a decrease in fertility. One of the factors in this direction will no doubt be of an economic character: the desire for a better standard of living which a large number of children tends to impede. *But these changes in old customs are slow and take many generations to evolve.*"

But, we are not dealing here in "generations." At best, it is one, or one-and-a-half generations. We are dealing with a situation that will occur in 30 to 50 years, in the lifetime of those among us who are young and who comprise more than half of the existing population.

Furthermore, most of the Arabs in Israel, including those in the territories, are farmers. To them a large number of children is not a burden but an asset. The children are a source of cheap farm-labor, as well as a way to bring in substantial income if they are sent to work in the cities.

In addition, the Israeli welfare policy encourages Arab fertility by paying monthly grants for each child, Jew and Arab alike. As for the immigration of Arabs from the West Bank, they usually return after they have earned enough money to buy a wife, as is the Moslem custom.

Thus, there is no probability that the demographic forecast as indicated in Table 1 will change noticeably in the period under consideration.

In spite of this, we must stress the great importance of Jewish settlement in Judea and Samaria, and the Gaza Strip. Only Jewish settlement in all parts of the Land of Israel will secure Jewish supremacy in the State of Israel.

It is, therefore, desirable to channel all available resources towards this aim, even if the goal of Jewish majority in these areas can not be reached at present. For while the Jews and Arabs live separately in their villages and towns, the Jewish character of Israel will be maintained as it is in Galilee, as long as there will be Jewish military and political rule in all the territories.

Now, let us examine the point of view of Liberals and Leftists in Israel who oppose the annexation of the West Bank and the Gaza Strip which are densely populated by Arabs.

In 1977, that area within the pre Six-Day War boundaries contained an Arab minority of 570,000 which is 15.6 per cent of the total population. The ratio between Jews and Arabs was 1:5.4.

This ratio is considered by those who are against annexations as "good," for it does not endanger the Jewish character of Israel.

Assuming the same birthrates of Jews and Arabs as before,

let us look at Table 2 which indicates the population growth in the "small" pre-1967 Israel.

Column A again shows the increase of Jews without immigration. Column B points out the increase of Jews with optimal immigration. Column C shows the natural increase of the Arabs within these borders.

The question arises whether in the future, the "good" ratio of 1 Arab to 5.4 Jews can be maintained in the "small" Israel. Using the same analytical method as we did in the case of Greater Israel, the number of Jews at the end of 20 years should be, according to Table 2: 1.2 million Arabs x 5.4 equaling 6.5 million Jews. Taking into account natural increase there will be only 4.3 million Jews — a deficiency of 2.2 millions.

This deficiency has to be made up during the first 20 years by an average net immigration (abstracting the returners) of 100,000 Jews per year.

In order to keep this rate another 20 years, the number of Jews 40 years from now should be, according to the Table, 2.5 million Arabs x 5.4 equaling 13.5 million Jews.

The number of Jews from natural increase at that time will be, provided the immigration quota of the first 20 years has been filled, 8.8 million Jews, i.e. a deficiency of 4.7 million Jews.

This deficiency must be made up, during the period that occurs 20 to 40 years from now, by an annual net immigration of over 200,000 Jews.

In a similar way, we shall find that in the period between 40 to 60 years, the deficiency will grow to 13.5 million Jews or, a required net yearly immigration of 650,000; again an absurd number. I have meticulously repeated this analysis only to emphasize that in the "small" Israel, of pre-1967 borders and with the small Arab minority, the present "good" ratio between Jews and Arabs also cannot be maintained at any time; or even stabilized. Table 2 shows the constant relative growth of the Arab population, until it reaches the line of parity with the Jews.

Here, I would like to mention one of the objections of the anti-annexationists: "We do not want to rule over one million Arabs."

Table 2 shows that in 20 years in the smaller Israel they will have to "rule" over 1.2 million; in 40 years over 2.5 million, and in 60 years over 5 million Arabs. As shown in Column A, Jewish supremacy in the pre-1967 Israel will end in about 85 years, if

2 ISRAEL OF THE PRE-1967 BORDERS
DEMOGRAPHICAL FORECAST-IN MILLIONS-

A JEWS, FROM NATURAL INCREASE, WITHOUT IMMIGRATION
B JEWS, FROM NATURAL INCREASE AND OPTIMAL IMMIGR.
C_1 ARABS, FR. NATURAL INCREASE

YEARS	A JEWS	C_1 ARABS		B JEWS
1977	3.07	0.57	13.6%	3.07
+ 20	4.3	1.2	21.5%	6.0
+ 40	6.1	2.5	29%	8.8
+ 60	8.4	5.0	37%	12.5
+ 80	11.6	9.9	46%	17.4
PARITY +100	15.7	19.3	55%	24 —
112 +120	21 —	37 —		32 — PARITY
+ 140	28 —	69 —		43 —
+ 160	37 —	125 —		57
+ 180	48 —	230 —		75 —

there will be no significant immigration. In a favorable situation of an optimal immigration, as shown in Column B, this fate will be delayed by another 25 years: The line will be reached in 110 years.

This leads us to the conclusion that both sides — those who are in favor of the annexation of the territories and those who prefer the "small" Israel on demographical grounds — are wrong. In both cases, the Jews will lose their majority and will become a minority and therefore they will lose the Jewish state. It will occur in the Greater Israel in 30 to 50 years; in the "small" Israel in 85 to 110 years.

The difference is about 60 years: Both time-spans are very short in the life of a nation. These events are bound to materialize in our own lifetime, or in that of our sons and daughters.

There are still some optimists in Israel who believe that a mass immigration of Jews will solve the demographical problem. That is just not so.

Even if it were possible to bring millions of Jews in a short time to Israel, the calculation proves that in this case, the line of parity will be postponed by two or three decades only.

Our problem resembles the classic mathematical exercise we learned in school.

Train A leaves the station at a certain hour and travels at a certain speed. Train B leaves at the same station at a later hour, but travels at a greater speed: When will train B overtake train A?

The Arab "train" in Israel is moving at a tremendous speed. It will inevitably overtake the much slower Jewish "train." After two thousand years of exile and dispersion among the nations, the Jewish people began a hundred years ago to return to their old homeland. With great effort and much sacrifice the Jews succeeded in those hundred years to rejuvenate and resettle the arid, neglected country.

In the four wars that claimed thousands of lives, the Jews renewed their sovereignty in the Land of their Fathers — a phenomenon in the history of the human race. Will brave endeavors, sacrifices, and beliefs in the Zionist dream come to an end in another hundred years? Was that pioneering just an heroic episode in the history of the Jewish people? Will it be then the end of Israel and the Jewish people?

Israel and the Jewish people must prevent this development at all costs.

But the demographic issue is not only a question of the relative numbers of Jews and Arabs. It is folly to assume that the Arabs of Israel will patiently wait a few decades until the supremacy of Israel falls into their hands like a ripe fruit. Long before the "line" of ethnic parity will be reached, the nationalistic pressure of a large Arab minority of millions will lead to an explosion — the beginnings of which we are already witnessing today.

6. THE JEWS ARE COMING

The resettlement of the Jews in the Land of Israel began one hundred years ago. I described the condition of the country in those days: Desolation, neglect, marshes, diseases and a high rate of mortality.

It is an historic fact that from the moment the Jews were exiled from the land nearly two thousand years ago, the Jewish return to the Holy Land never ceased.

While the motivation for this coming back to the Land in previous centuries was mostly religious, it should be remembered that for Jews, their nationality, religion and history form a single entity.

For generations, Jews made attempts to launch a mass return to the Land of Israel. They failed because of unfavorable political conditions. However, Jews living in the Diaspora never gave up nor accepted their fate. Every Passover eve they chanted the prayer: "Next Year in Jerusalem." Zion, Jerusalem, Israel are the most meaningful words in the Holy Scriptures, the Bible and Prayerbooks. Even Jewish children were infused with the knowledge that there is a Promised Land and its capital is Jerusalem. They were taught that someday the ingathering of the exiles will commence and Jews will come home. From the age of three, children heard stories from their teachers about the Land of Israel, the Judges of Israel, the Kings of Israel, the heros of Israel, as well as the destruction of the First and Second Temples and the Wars of Israel.

At the end of the Nineteenth Century, a wave of liberalism,

which included a desire for national self-determination, swept Europe. Jews began to organize. This time, their motivation was not religious. Now, they were moved by nationalistic feelings. True, they wanted to escape anti-Semitism, persecution and poverty. But above all, they wanted to live in freedom and dignity.

Many immigrated to the United States. But an idealistic minority organized themselves into a movement called BILU and went to the Land of Israel.

From its inception, this movement did not contain political aspirations. They left Europe to become farmers in the Land of Israel.

The resettlement was made possible by the generous philanthropic aid of Baron Edmond de Rothschild who established a financial and administrative organization to support these first settlers.

This settlement which occurred before the founding of Zionism went on for thirty years. It came to an abrupt halt at the beginning of World War I.

During this brief period, more than thirty Jewish "colonies" (villages) were established. The first Jewish urban settlements were erected. Outside the city walls of Old Jerusalem, a Jewish suburb was started which later became modern Jerusalem. A Jewish suburb outside of Jaffa grew into the metropolis of Tel Aviv. Haifa, on the slopes of Mount Carmel, was built and populated by Jews.

The solid foundations of the future, modern Jewish State, were laid in those first thirty years of Jewish settlement. Today's much-in-demand Jaffa oranges had their roots in the groves planted in those early days. In Rishon Le Zion, a wine press was built. The Herzlia High School was opened. An agricultural school was set up in Mikveh Israel. Medical clinics began functioning. Industrial enterprises were created.

But most important was the rejuvenation of the ancient Hebrew language, the Language of the Bible. From kindergarten through high school, children were taught in modern, conversational Hebrew. Newspapers were printed in Hebrew. Theatrical groups performed in the revived language.

The Hashomer (Watchmen) Society was organized. This group of armed Jewish mounted volunteer police guarded the homes and agricultural settlements of the new Jewish farmers against Arab raids.

All these developments took place with the knowledge of Turkish authorities. The Turks had some doubts about this pioneering venture. Obviously, the nationalistic aspects of Jewish resettlement did not escape them. But on the other hand, the Turks were interested in the development of this neglected area, as well as in the investments of Baron de Rothschild.

In those days, the Arabs saw no reason to oppose the new Jewish settlers. Thanks to the Jews, many *fellahin* were employed on the new farms and orange groves. Arab craftsmen found employment in the new cities.

Most of the first Jewish settlers were Russian and Rumanian. They lived in Palestine under the protection of the consulates of their former countries.

Therefore, at the outbreak of World War I, the Turks considered them alien subjects and they were ordered to leave the country. Most of them moved to Egypt.

7. THE ZIONISTS ARE COMING

The Zionist movement was founded in 1897.

Dr. Theodor Herzl, a Jewish journalist from Vienna and an author of a book entitled *Der Judenstaat* (The Jewish State), invited prominent leaders of World Jewry to Basel, Switzerland, for the first Zionist Congress. The Congress created a political movement known as Zionism. Its aim was to create a Jewish state in the ancient land of the Jews: The Land of Israel.

For generations, Jews were dispersed among Christians and Moslems. They always were a minority, an alien element in religion, nationality and race. Because of religious fanaticism, economic jealousy or xenophobia, Jews were humiliated, persecuted and murdered. They would receive various short periods of grace and security because of their finanical services to kings and princes.

For centuries, religious Jews lived in a closed society. They yearned for the Messiah to lead them from slavery to freedom and to bring them from exile to the Land of their Fathers.

The French Revolution, the rise of Napoleon and the new liberal spirit that swept Europe raised new hopes for Jews. Many of them became influenced by these progressive movements. They gave up their traditional religious heritage and turned to secularism. They believed that liberalism and progressivism would also bring the long-coveted human rights and equality to Jews, too!

Many obtained higher education and became part of the general Christian society. They became active in the spheres of art, science, literature and politics. They were imbued with the optimism that a new dawn in the life of mankind was at hand. They felt that the walls separating mankind were falling down and that prejudice against Jews would disappear.

Soon, however, the Jews woke up to reality. They found that under the thin veneer of liberalism nothing had changed. Even the most liberal and educated Christian remained a Jew-hater.

At the end of the Nineteenth Century, the Dreyfus Affair stirred Europe. It was a reminder that anti-Semitism was unchanged. Dreyfus was a Jewish Captain in the French army. He was falsely accused of betraying military secrets to the enemy. Despite lack of evidence, a French court-martial sentenced him to life imprisonment on Devil's Island.

Covering the trial as a journalist, Dr. Herzl witnessed the humiliating ceremony of the removing of the captain's insignia, as well as the breaking of his sword. Until that very incident, Dr. Herzl also belonged to the group of assimilated, intellectual Jews. He, like many other members of the Russian Jewish intelligentsia, came to the conclusion that Jews stood no chance of living in freedom, equality and dignity as a minority among the nations. They must have a country of their own, in their ancient land. Thus was born the idea of political Zionism.

Here I wish to point out that Zionism is definitely not a movement of Jewish refugees fleeing pogroms or poverty. Zionism is a movement of proud Jews who rebelled against a life of humiliation and discrimination. Zionism is a movement of freedom.

National freedom and dignity motivated Zionism from the outset.

33

The new Jewish immigrants from the Soviet Union are the best examples that Zionism was, and still is, the driving force of Jews in the Diaspora. After the glorious victory of Israel in the Six-Day War in 1967, dormant Jewish national feelings stirred among Russian Jews. They demanded and fought for the right to emigrate from Russia and join their brethren in Israel. They did not do this because of economical or political reasons. Many Russian immigrants belonged to the privileged classes in the U.S.S.R. They were professors, artists, engineers and other professionals. Their motivation was nationalistic. They wanted to live among their own people in dignity, something which was denied them in the country of their birth. Jews are considered as an alien element, not only in the West, but also in Communist countries.

The Zionist organization came into being at a time when Colonial powers were maneuvering for "spheres of influence." It was quite natural that they tried to achieve the establishment of a Jewish State by diplomatic means. They appealed to leading personalities, statesmen, kings and emperors. Pressure was exerted on the Turkish Sultan to grant the Jews a charter for settlement in Palestine. The Ottoman Treasury was empty. Although the Turks were tempted, they turned down all appeals because of their fear of political repercussions.

The founders of Zionism — Dr. Herzl, Max Nordau, Menahem Ussishkin — were born in the Nineteenth Century. They were all brought up on humanistic ideals and were imbued with the liberal spirit of their day. They wholeheartedly believed that Jewish settlement in Palestine would not only liberate the Jewish people, but would also bring prosperity to the Arab inhabitants of the Holy Land. All of them, without exception, had no doubt that the Arabs would sympathetically welcome the return of the Jews to their homeland.

The Zionists felt that the Arab minority would have equal rights in the Jewish State. This principle recurs in all the writings of Zionism: The Arabs will be better off in a Jewish State. They belong to the same Semitic race. They shall be treated as equals.

In those days, the Zionists hoped in a short time to bring a million or two million East European Jews to Palestine and establish a Jewish majority — a Jewish State.

The Zionists wanted to prove that it is possible to treat a

minority without any discrimination and persecution. Israel will be a "light to the nations" and serve as an example for a democratic, progressive state, where all citizens have equal rights and opportunities, regardless of religion, race or nationality.

It should be remembered that all these liberal ideas had been formulated in the previous century when the Arab population in Palestine was exceedingly small and the Land itself was barren. If those conditions had prevailed, things might have indeed developed according to the script of the Founding Fathers of Zionism.

Ever since the Jews were exiled from their homeland and dispersed among the nations, they tried on several occasions to regain political independence. Time and again, the conditions were against them. After the fall of Rome, the Byzantine Christians ruled Palestine. Later the country was conquered by fanatic Moslems who rode in from the desert. Then came the Crusaders, no less fanatic. In the Fifteenth Century, the Land was conquered by the Ottoman Turks who were feared in Europe and who were stopped only at the gates of Vienna.

At last, in the beginning of the Century, political conditions became more favorable for Zionist aspirations. When World War I broke out, the Zionist movement supported and aided the Allies. Jewish regiments were formed and incorporated into the British Army. Jews in Palestine collaborated with British intelligence.

In 1917, Dr. Chaim Weizmann, the foremost leader of the Zionist movement, whose chemical invention helped the Allied war effort, obtained a written promise from the British government to support the establishment of a "Jewish Homeland in Palestine." The document was signed by the then British Foreign Secretary Lord Balfour and is known as the Balfour Declaration.

After the Allied victory, the Ottoman Empire was divided among the victors:

In the Paris Peace Conference of 1919, France obtained the northern section of the Syrian Province. There, she established two protectorates: Syria, which was Moslem; and Lebanon whose inhabitants were Christian and Moslem.

Britain received the southern part of the Syrian Province

known as Palestine. It was a Mandate from the League of Nations so that Britain could implement the Balfour Declaration by establishing a Jewish National Homeland in Palestine.

It is important to remember that the Mandate for the establishment of a Jewish Homeland in Palestine included the territory of Transjordan, i.e. the present-day Kingdom of Jordan, which also historically belonged to the Jewish people.

Following the ratification of the Balfour Declaration by the League of Nations, Jewish immigration and settlement of the Land were vigorously renewed.

8. ARAB NATIONALISM

Present-day Arab nationalism is extremist, aggressive and full of self-importance. It encompasses the whole Arab world.

One of its aims is the destruction of the State of Israel. While the annihilation of Israel is their first step, their aspirations are more ambitious.

Arab nationalism is a relatively new phenomenon. Until the fall of the Ottoman Empire, there were no Arab nationalist, separatist movements. This contrasted sharply with the Greek, Bulgarian, Albanian nationalist movements in that very same Turkish Empire. The Turkish Sultan also held the title of Khaliff of the Devouts — the spiritual head of all Moslems.

Arab Moslems throughout the Turkish Province considered themselves loyal subjects of the Sultan who held reign in Constantinople.

In the Turkish Empire, there were no Arab freedom movements similar to those of the Serbs, Croatians, Poles and Czechs who were active in the Austro-Hungarian Empire. There were no such movements in the Syrian-Palestinian Province of the Turkish Empire. There were no underground groups and no activities calling for independence. The population of this Province was not interested in any "liberation." They did not consider themselves as national entities in need of self-determination. The existing situation seemed to them quite normal and satisfactory.

However, a nationalistic movement existed in the Arab

world in the semi-independent Kingdom of Egypt. This movement was not Arab-nationalist, but Egyptian-nationalist. It was directed against the British imperialists who controlled Egypt from 1883-1945.

The Egyptians are devout Moslems who speak Arabic. However, they do not consider themselves Arabs, but as the descendants of the Egyptians of antiquity.

For hundreds of years, Egypt has been the leading and most advanced nation in the Arab World and the center of Arab-Moslem learning and tradition. Despite some isolationist groups, Egypt, therefore, will not renounce its leading role in the Pan-Arabic and Pan-Islamic struggle.

Another province in the Ottoman Empire was Hejaz. This was a region along the eastern coast of the Red Sea. Hejaz is mostly populated by Bedouin tribes and includes the two sacred towns of Islam: Mecca and Medina. Here lived Mohammed, the founder and Prophet of Islam.

At the beginning of World War I the nominal ruler of Hejaz was the "Sheriff of Mecca," a viceroy. His name was Hussein Ibn Ali of the Hashemite family which considered themselves descendants of Mohammed.

During World War I, a British agent and adventurer, Colonel T.E. Lawrence, persuaded Sheriff Hussein and other desert Sheikhs — with a great deal of gold — to sabotage the narrow track of "Hejaz Railway" which ran from Damascus to Medina. Their goal was to disrupt movement and supplies behind the Turkish lines.

These acts of sabotage, perpetrated by several hundred Bedouin, were later blown completely out of all proportion. In the best tradition of Oriental fantasy, these skirmishes were translated into a "wide-scale" Arab revolt against the Turks. Lawrence, who wished to glorify himself, purposely created and nurtured this legend which later became an "historical fact."

It would be erroneous to attach any military importance to these acts of sabotage, or to consider them as an expression of an Arab uprising. At the most, they were actions taken to advance the dynastic interests of the Hashemites.

And indeed, this family knew how to turn the miniscule help it contributed to the British war effort into good use. With Britain's help, Feisal, Sheriff Hussein's son, became the Arabs' main spokesman at the Paris Peace Conference. Later, the British made him King of Syria. But when the French drove him out of the area, the British then set him up as King of Iraq, under the protectorate of Britain, of course.

The British gave his brother Abdullah the Emirate of Transjordan which literally was torn away from the British Mandate of Palestine. The latter was to have been the Jewish Homeland.

These two brothers were unknown to the Syrian Arabs. They were outsiders, planted there by the British solely because of the British colonial interests.

An important fact to remember is that at the Paris Conference in 1919, Feisal Ibn Hussein met with the Zionist leader, Dr. Chaim Weizmann. The two reached a mutual understanding regarding their aspirations. In his famous letter to Weizmann Feisal expressed his good wishes to the Zionist effort. He hoped that both peoples would cooperate.

9. THE ARABISTS

At the end of World War I, the Zionist movement had reason to be optimistic. More than at any time previously, it looked forward to the realization of its hopes and ideals.

On the one hand, Great Britain's generous promise to support the establishment of a Jewish National Home was embodied in the Balfour Declaration. To demonstrate her sincere intentions, the British government nominated Sir Herbert Samuel, a British-Jewish statesman, to be the first High Commissioner of Palestine.

Evident also was the initial sympathetic and positive attitude of the Arab leaders who saw the Jews as being a progressive Western nation, with advanced technological knowledge and considerable financial means. All this, they believed, would advance the development of their own backward, but new, Arab states.

But the British-Arab-Jewish idyll did not last very long. It came to an end soon.

It is difficult to point out with any degree of certainty the objective and rational reasons that brought about the drastic change in the tri-lateral relations. No doubt, the reasons were not always rational. Certainly they were not predictable. Even the historians are not in agreement about the factors that caused the deterioration in the British-Arab-Jewish relations.

Probably one of the reasons for the change of mind was the realization by the Palestinian Arabs that they were about to lose their supremacy in Palestine because of the influx of the Jewish immigrants.

The British, on their part, probably realized that the great momentum of Zionist settlement was moving quite beyond their policy. They saw that the Jews interpreted the Balfour Declaration more comprehensively than the British government really intended.

Consequently, the Mandatory authorities initiated a policy of containing Zionist momentum in various ways. For instance, it granted immigration permits to Jews, only "according to the country's economic possibilities." This was a very arbitrary regulation.

In those days in Palestine, it was generally assumed that the local British civil servants had been those who incited Arabs against the Jews and that they did so contrary to the directions of the central government in London. There is no doubt that the civil servants in Palestine did not sympathize with Zionism and the Jews in general. Among other reasons, the Jews did not comply with the pattern that the British had become accustomed to as a result of centuries of colonial rule.

The Jews were not "natives." In India and Africa, the British civil servants dominated the local population. But that was just not possible with the Jews.

What was even more infuriating to the British was what they considered the Jews' arrogance. From their first day in the country, Jews believed they were the inheritors of British rule.

The Arabs, on the other hand, conformed to the colonial pattern and to the tradition of Oriental courtesy and exotic and submissive hospitality. No wonder the British administration preferred the Arabs and acted accordingly.

Yet, based on the authority of an abundance of documents and evidence, it was not local British civil servants that dictated the anti-Jewish policy in Palestine. It was the British Foreign Office in London. That Office was manned then, and probably is today, by a majority of "Arabists." They preached that preference of the Arab cause would advance the interest of Britain. Supporting the Zionist effort might antagonize the Arab World against England. Of course, not all British statesmen were in agreement with the anti-Zionist Arabists in the Foreign Office. Both in the Government and in Parliament, Zionism has always had a number of friends and sympathizers, especially among the English people. The Zionist leaders counted on these friends. Both a moderate leader like Dr. Weizmann and a "hawk" like Ze'ev Jabotinsky believed in Britain almost to the expiration of the British Mandate. In spite of Britain's behavior, almost all the Jewish leaders felt that England was an ally and friend.

Indeed, during the first years of Mandatory rule Britain facilitated Jewish immigration to Palestine. The British did not stop the Jews from building cities, villages, factories and cultural institutions.

However, British support was only passive. The English administration did not put up a development budget for the new immigrants to Palestine, as they had done with other developing countries. The government did not allot one of the millions of acres of government lands to the Jews. Each plot of land that was settled by Jews had to be purchased in cash raised by World Jewry.

What was built in Israel was erected with Jewish toil and effort. People might argue about the reasons for Arab-Jewish enmity. The fact is that already in 1921, only two years after renewed Jewish immigration, the first Arab anti-Jewish riots broke out.

The foremost agitator and inciter of the 1921 riots — as well as of all the later riots — had been Haj Amin El Husseini, a member of an influential Arab family. This inciter, who was sentenced to prison, was nominated by the British High Commissioner to be the Grand Mufti of Jerusalem, religious head of the Moslem Arab community. This was done in the true tradition of the Colonial Administration.

In his role as the Grand Mufti, Husseini became the chief mouthpiece and authoritative leader of the Palestine Arabs. For twenty-five years, until the end of World War II, the Mufti waged a venomous propaganda war against Zionism and the Jewish people. It was the Mufti who time and time again instigated bloody riots. That role has now been taken over by Yassir Arafat, leader of the PLO.

The Mufti was not only a Jew-hater, he was also an enemy of the British. When Adolf Hitler appeared on the scene, Husseini became his fervent admirer and personal adviser in actions against the "common enemy"! The Jews. During World War II, Husseini recruited Moslem regiments who fought alongside the Nazi hordes. In fiery exhortations on Radio Berlin, he incited the Arab Moslems against Britain and the United States.

It did not take long for the Jews to realize that they would have to accomplish their Zionist program — the establishment of the Jewish State — in spite of Arab protests and active resistance, as well as negative British policy. Therefore, the Jews of Palestine organized armed underground groups called the Haganah (Defense). Until the end of British rule, Haganah defended the Jewish community against Arab armed attacks. It was Haganah that contributed to the security and strengthening of the Jewish population which had grown to a half a million.

For fifty years, Jewish farmers in Palestine often had to toil their land as did their Biblical ancestors: 'with a plow in one hand, the sword in the other.' Today, it is a tractor and a gun . . .

The Arab refusal to recognize the rights of the Jewish people to Palestine — the Land of Israel — never diminished. Even today, sixty-three years after the Balfour Declaration, this Arab enmity is even more intransigent and unresolved than ever.

What the Arabs resented most of all was constant Jewish immigration (the aliya). The Arabs saw in aliya — and rightly so — the decisive factor in the development of a Jewish majority and hegemony in Palestine.

But one must not forget that the Arabs already had received their share of the Turkish legacy: Syria, Lebanon, Iraq, Hejaz (Saudi Arabia). What the Arabs obviously want now is their share of the land of the Jews.

Arab resistance of the common heritage was not the main cause of concern to the new and growing Jewish community. Those who represented the real danger to Zionism were the British Arabists in the Foreign Office whose influence was getting stronger. These Arabists were persuaded by Arab arguments. They increasingly limited the number of Jewish immigration permits, the "certificates," as they were called.

Following prolonged Arab riots, the British decided to put a complete stop to the Jewish immigration to Palestine. Thus, they "brutally" violated the Balfour Declaration given to the Jewish people by the British, as well as the Mandate given to Britain by the League of Nations.

In 1939, the British Government issued a "White Paper" which stipulated that Jewish immigration should come to a complete stop. It said that the Jews should receive no more than ten thousand (10,000) certificates per year in the next five years. But considering the plight of the Jews trying to escape Nazi persecution, the British Government would allow an additional immigration of twenty-five thousand (25,000) Jews.

This was one of the most terrible and tragic decrees proclaimed against the Jewish people in their long history. After all, this was the time of Hitler's Nazi regime; the annexation of European countries, and the persecution of Jews and other racial minorities.

Britain's White Paper was virtually a death sentence for millions of European Jews.

Today, forty years later, the State of Israel is established; but British influence in the Middle East has all but disappeared.

It could be assumed, therefore, that the Arabists would also vanish together with Colonial Imperialism. But what actually happened was quite different. The spirit of pro-Arabism is still very much alive. It has passed from the British Foreign Office to the American State Department. It flourishes at the Brookings Institute. The pro-Arab circles in the United States wish to move back the hands of the clock of history. They make supreme efforts to establish a "homeland for the Palestinians," located in the very heart of the Jewish State. This act can have only one aim: The destruction of Israel. In the past, pro-Arab civil servants fought against Jewish immigration. Today, they wage an all-out war against Jewish settlements being set up in a Jewish State.

But our position today differs vastly from our position under the Mandate. Today, Israel is a sovereign state and possesses a formidable military force. If the Jews managed to overcome British schemes, Israel shall be able to withstand State Department plots.

10. THE ESTABLISHMENT OF ISRAEL

The White Paper, whose aim was to put a stop to Jewish immigration, to end Zionism and to dash hopes of establishing a Jewish state, caused a drastic change in the relations between the Jewish community in Palestine and the British Administration. There was no cooperation with the Mandatory authorities; only an active struggle for the continuation of Jewish immigration in every way possible.

Haganah, which had fought Arab "fedayeen" terrorists, now organized for a new mission: the illegal immigration of Jews to Palestine. This immigration was named "Aliya Bet" (Immigration B).

Haganah members were sent to Europe. There, they organized groups of Jewish refugees and brought them to European ports. From there, the refugees were placed onto old and decrepit and overcrowded vessels. The ships moved towards the shores of the Promised Land. Near the coast, they were transferred at night into boats and put ashore. Here the immigrants were received by other Haganah personnel who quickly transported them to safe places.

All this was done under the noses of British patrol boats trying to intercept these immigrants.

In time, the British perfected their tactics and succeeded in intercepting the immigrant ships on the high seas. British destroyers would overtake the ships and direct them to the port of Haifa. These immigrants then were transferred to naval vessels and sent to the island of Cyprus. There, they were kept in detention camps for several years until the State of Israel was established and opened its gates.

The heroic epic of Aliya Bet and the Ma'apilim (illegal immigrants) has been immortalized in books and films. One such ship was the "Struma" which the British sunk with all its passengers aboard. Another famous ship was the "Exodus." At the end of 1939, the British demonstrated their perfidious indifference when they forced immigrant ships to sail back to their ports of departure.

The desperate refugees, fleeing from the Nazis, had suffered for days and weeks in overloaded ships. They lacked food, drink and sanitary installations. These terribly unfortunate people were sent back by the British — straight into Hitler's gas chambers.

The Jewish people will never forget these inhuman acts.

Today the United States as well as many European countries sell weapons to the Arab states for billions of dollars. These governments profess to be friends of Israel, although they know that the Arab states are at war with Israel and that the main purpose of these weapons is to destroy Israel.

The sale of armaments to the Arabs is, in my opinion, not unlike providing Hitler with Ziklon poison gas which suffocated Jews in the gas chambers.

While the Haganah continued its action of bringing in immigrants, and thus confronted the Mandatory Authorities, the leaders of the Zionist Organization did not break off their relations with the British Government in London. The Zionists hoped that their lobbying would bring about a change in the British stand regarding Jewish immigration.

But there were other, more hawkish circles in Palestine who thought otherwise. They now considered Britain to be Zionism's enemy. These groups formed two underground organizations. Both were more extremist than the Haganah: One was Irgun Tzvi Leumi (ETZEL) which was later to be commanded by

Menahem Begin, now the Prime Minister of Israel. The other group was "Freedom Fighters of Israel" (LEHI), known as the "Stern Gang." These two organizations declared war on the British Administration of Palestine and sabotaged British civil and military installations.

With the outbreak of World War II, the underground groups suspended their anti-British actions. An unofficial truce was declared. The Jewish community in Israel supported the British against the common enemy — Nazi Germany. A Jewish Brigade was incorporated into the British Army and many Irgun and Haganah members served in its ranks, as they did in other British fighting units.

After the war, the world changed its image and its values. Nations disappeared from the face of the earth. The Eastern European countries turned into the satellites of the Soviet Union. Millions of displaced persons sought their relatives and their former homes. The world then learned about the crematoria of Auschwitz, as well as the gruesome fact that Six Million Jews were massacred in the Holocaust.

But the British were unmoved. They returned to their interrupted pre-World War II policy. Again, they began to carry out the anti-Jewish policy of the infamous White Paper.

The Jewish underground organizations now renewed their activities with more vigor. This time, Haganah joined the activist forces. The stubborn fight against the British lasted for two more years until London gave up trying to find a solution to the Arab-Jewish conflict and decided to return the Mandate of Palestine to the United Nations.

In November, 1947, the United Nations General Assembly voted overwhelmingly to partition Palestine into two independent states, one Jewish and one Arabic.

On May 14, 1948, the British Mandate in Palestine came to an end. On that very same day, the National Jewish Council proclaimed the establishment of the Jewish State, to be called Israel. David Ben-Gurion became its first Prime Minister and Dr. Chaim Weizmann its first President. The very next morning, the armies of Egypt, Syria, Lebanon, Jordan and Iraq invaded the territory that the U.N. proclaimed as the Jewish State. Their

45

war planes bombed Tel Aviv and other cities and towns. Thus began the first war between Israel and the Arab states, a conflict known as the Israel War of Independence. This battle lasted until the end of the year. Despite a lack of military and economic organization, Israel repelled regular Arab armies. In the War, the Jewish State gained more land than originally alloted to her by the U.N. Partition Plan.

A cease-fire agreement was signed on the Island of Rhodes by Israel and the Arab states. The mediator was Dr. Ralph Bunche of the United Nations. This cease-fire lasted for nearly 20 years.

An unforseen consequence of the Israel War of Independence was that between three to four hundred thousand Arabs abandoned their homes in Palestine. They fled from those areas which contained mixed Arab-Jewish populations. They left because they were instructed to do so by their leaders who were convinced that the regular armies of Egypt, Syria, Lebanon, Jordan and Iraq would destroy Israel which still was attempting to organize itself. The liquidation of Jews would take about two weeks, the Arab leaders predicted.

The Arab civilian population would have been a hindrance to the advancing armies. Their leaders promised them huge spoils: Jewish lands, homes and women. But as it turned out, Israel defeated the five invading Arab armies. The Arabs who deserted their homes were not allowed to return. These are the "Palestinian refugees." Today, more than 30 years later, most of them are still living in misery in camps in neighboring Syria, Jordan and Lebanon.

Soon the abandoned Arab homes were occupied by Jewish immigrants from the Arab countries of North Africa. These Jews left behind their homes and property in Morocco, Algeria, Tunisia and Yemen. In 1967, the President of Egypt, Gamal Abdul Nasser, closed the Straits of Tiran, the entrance of the Gulf of Eilat, which was Israel's gateway to the Red Sea and the Indian Ocean. Egypt, Syria and Jordan mobilized their armies against Israel. The Jewish State again was forced to fight.

The campaign lasted only six days and is known as the Six-Day War. The Arab armies were overwhelmingly defeated and Israel took the Sinai Peninsula, the Golan Heights and the West Bank.

Today, the Arabs and the foreign media call these areas

"Arab occupied territories." But Jews everywhere, and Israelis in particular, see these territories as liberated, Jewish historical lands — which Israel decisively now possesses.

The presentation of the true and objective facts in the last few chapters should be a guideline for every sincere man and woman to understand the Arab-Israel conflict; especially the younger generation whose views are distorted by Arab propaganda fueled by millions of petro-dollars and by a media alien to Israel.

11. ISRAEL AND THE ARAB WORLD

Four Arab-Israel battles followed that first Israel War of Independence in 1948: the 1956 Sinai Campaign; the 1967 Six-Day War; the 1970 War of Attrition; and the 1973 Yom Kippur War. In all these clashes, the Arabs attempted again and again to destroy the State of Israel and drive the Jews into the sea.

For three decades, Israeli leaders tried to reach agreement with their Arab neighbors. They were unsuccessful because for many years, the Arabs have been nurtured on hatred against the Jews. This hatred has become an inherent part of their mentality.

Why is Arab hatred so deeply rooted?
What are the true motives of the Arabs?
What motivates the Jews?
Is there any way at all that the conflict between Arab and Jew can be ended?

Give Israel the option: genuine peace with the Arabs bound by peace treaties in return for withdrawals from various parts of Israel; or continued enmity of the Arabs, including the danger of war — many Israelies would still be prepared to carry on the fight. They feel that the fulfillment of Zionism is the realization of our eternal right to the Land of Israel.

But let us consider the viewpoints of those Israelis who believe that in exchange for territorial concessions, it is possible to come to terms with the Arabs.

These Israelis make up various factions. There are those prepared for far-reaching concessions, but only in return for "true-peace." There are those ready to make concessions, in return only for cessation of the state of war. There are those that are willing to give up Sinai, but not the West Bank — Judea and Samaria. There are those who are ready to surrender the Golan Heights, too. There are the Communists who urge the return of all the territories, including East Jerusalem, and without any condition. There is no end to the number of nuances of those who "are prepared to . . ."

Without being drawn into dovish or hawkish viewpoints, have we any alternative? Is it really possible to make peace with Arabs in return for any kind of territorial withdrawal? Can we at least reach actual non-belligerency? Every one will agree with the following premise:

In order to achieve peace, both sides must be interested in peace.

As far as Israel is concerned, there is not the shadow of a doubt that it wants to live in peace. Peace is essential to Israel so that it can develop, thrive and absorb new immigrants; so that its sons will not fall in battle; so that its civilians will not perpetually live under the threat of annihilation.

But what about the Arabs? Do they, too, need peace like we do? The answer is no.

The Arabs do not need peace with Israel. The Arabs already have peace with the Jewish State. Israel does not wage war with them. It has no intention of destroying the Arab states. The present state of war is one-sided. Israel does not impose an embargo on the Arabs. It does not inflict terror upon them. The Arabs, however, harm Israel. They dispatch fully-armed terrorists against men, women and children. They organize a world economic boycott against Israel. They threaten it with total war and destruction.

Some say the Arabs need peace to develop and rehabilitate their countries and raise the standard of living of their citizens.

The question must be asked: Who prevents the Arabs from directing all their energies to the development of their economically poor countries, instead of creating armies poised against Israel?

The Arabs can disarm. Israel has no wish whatsoever to conquer Cairo or Damascus; no desire to be responsible for forty million undernourished Egyptians.

True, the Arabs want to regain the lands of Israel occupied in 1967. But will not the Sahara Desert be sufficient for the Egyptians? Is the Sinai Desert so vital to Eygpt's needs? Has Syria exploited the millions of uncultivated acres along the river Euphrates? Can she not get along without the Golan Heights? Is it worth the sacrifice of billions of dollars, tens of thousands of soldiers, as well as the destruction of their towns and villages to regain these areas?

Let us suppose for a moment that the real object of the Arabs is to liberate the West Bank and the Gaza Strip; to establish what they define as "the legitimate rights of the Palestinians."

The world must note that all the occupied territories were in the hands of the Arabs from 1948 to 1967. During this twenty-year period, why didn't they initiate the "rights of the Palestinians" in these areas? Why didn't they establish a "Palestinian State"? Why didn't they transfer the refugees from their camps to residential homes in this proposed state?

The problem of self-determination of the Palestinians in these areas did not arise at all when the West Bank was part of the Kingdom of Jordan and the Gaza Strip was held by Egypt. The residents of these areas who today call themselves "Palestinians" considered themselves loyal subjects and an integral part of Jordan or Egypt.

Moreover, beginning from the day of the establishment of the State of Israel in 1948 and until the Six-Day War in 1967, hardly a day passed without terrorist Fedayeen penetrating Israeli territory. The "Arab Army of Liberation" was set up in the Gaza Strip by the agitator Ahmed Shukeiry. Twice, Egypt closed the Straits of Tiran on the Gulf of Eilat to Israeli commercial shipping. To withhold water for Israeli agriculture and to starve Israel, Syria dug a channel to divert the Jordan River near its source on Mount Hermon. Why was this tremendous united Arab struggle waged against Israel?

Let us assume that Israel hands over all the territories it occupied in the Six-Day War to the Arabs. In addition, Israel will

49

allow a certain number of Palestinian refugees to return to the homes and villages they abandoned in 1948. Would that resolve the conflict once and for all? The answer unequivocally is no.

Some refugee organizations and their leaders would gladly assume control of the areas which Israel would evacuate, provided Egypt and Jordan would agree to this, which is doubtful. And there is still another obstacle — and that is "The Palestinian Covenant." This covenant, ratified by all Arab states, specifies that a "secular Palestinian State," meaning an Arab state, must be established in the area of the present Jewish State of Israel. It declares that Jewish immigration to this State must be stopped; and that Israelis born here after 1918 will be expelled from Palestine.

These conditions mean the end of a Jewish State in Israel. Not even the most dovish element of the Israeli public will accept it.

The Arabs, of course, are aware of this, but they have no reason to renounce it. Nor are they compelled to do so. While they will take any territory we hand over to them, such as the Sinai, they will, at the same time, continue to demand more and more. The conflict will go on.

What then is the real objective of the Arabs?
Is it to retrieve the occupied territories?
Is it to establish a "Palestinian Homeland"?
Is it to bring the Palestinian refugees back to Israel?

On the day the State of Israel was founded, the territories were in Arab hands. Not one single refugee existed.

Why then did five Arab armies attack Israel on the following day?

Obviously the Arab states rejected the establishment of a Jewish State in the midst of an Arab region.

After the Jewish State had become an accomplished fact, with a cease-fire agreement signed on Rhodes, the battle cry and the terror acts of the Arabs were directed towards one aim: To force Israel to allow the Palestinian refugees to return to their old homes and villages.

But can it be that this Arab struggle is conducted for the sake of the brotherly love of the refugees? The fact that these refugees are being held by their brothers for years in dilapidated camps under inferior makeshift conditions is in striking contrast to post- World War II Europe, where millions of refugees have long since been rehabilitated and absorbed into the social and economic life of their new land. This is proof of the total indifference the Arabs have for the fate of their "brother" refugees.

The refugees are not the cause of the Arab-Israel conflict. They are used by the Arab states as a political instrument against Israel.

Immediately after the Six-Day War of 1967, when the West Bank and the Gaza Strip fell under Israeli control, the Arab refugees transformed themselves into a "Palestinian nation." They organized militant terrorist groups, such as the PLO. Led by Yassir Arafat, they now claim that these terrorists are an integral part of a Palestinian Arab State, also comprising the present State of Israel.

All Arab states constantly threaten Israel with war unless it withdraws from the territories and unless a Palestinian state is established. Most countries in the West and the East support this Arab claim. The "legitimate rights of the Palestinians" have become the crux of the conflict in world politics.

But is it really for the sake of the "Palestinians" that the Arab world endeavors to establish such a State? Can it be of such vital importance to distant Arab countries like Algeria, Libya, Iraq, that they are prepared to sacrifice their sons and daughters for it?

In his dramatic visit to Jerusalem, Anwar Sadat, the President of Egypt, himself considered a "moderate," declared that the "heart of the conflict," is the "Palestinian homeland." Unless this problem is resolved, he says, there will not be peace in the Middle East. In fact, he adds, this problem was the stumbling block to all subsequent peace negotiations. But is the establishment of a state for the Palestinians such a vital issue for Egypt whose real problem is how to feed and provide housing and jobs for 40 million people whose population quickly multiplies?

The stubborn attitude of Egypt in the Egyptian-Israeli

peace negotiations indicates that Egypt must have a different motivation.

We should also remember that the PLO was cruelly suppressed in 1970 by King Hussein's Arab Legions. In the "Black September" days of that year, thousands of Palestinian guerrillas were killed and the rest expelled from Jordan.

Moreover, in Lebanon, where the Christian Lebanese were attacked by the Moslem Palestinians, the Syrian Moslem Army intervened, supporting the Lebanese.

The Palestinian problem is used by the Arab states for their own political aims. Without their backing, the PLO has no political or military standing whatsoever.

The question of whether there exists a "Palestinian nation," or a "Palestinian entity," is quite irrelevant. In the event of an Israeli withdrawal, it will not be the U.S. nor Israel who will decide if the West Bank becomes a "Palestinian Homeland." It is almost certain that this territory would be partitioned between Syria and Jordan, or incorporated in "Greater Syria." One result for sure is that Soviet "advisors" would get that much closer to Tel Aviv and Jerusalem.

Conclusion:

The heart of the Arab-Israel conflict is not the establishment of a Palestinian Homeland, nor the situation of the refugees. It is rather the compulsive, irrational and uncompromising Arab desire to remove the Jewish State from the "Dar el Islam," the Islamic sphere, and from Jerusalem. This can only be achieved by the physical destruction of Israel.

12. CONFRONTATION

At times, man's nature makes it difficult for him to face the harsh truth. The conclusions we offered in the previous chapter are indeed cruel. Some people will say the situation we described is desperate: If there is no hope for peace with the Arabs, then we are destined to live forever next to neighbors who are our enemies. We will, therefore, have to make more sacrifices. These people say there must be a better way.

Man also is optimistic by nature. In every person there exists a mechanism that suppresses the unpleasant things. Thanks to this mechanism we succeed in building for ourselves a beautiful world founded on illusions and wishful thinking. We hide under the cloak of rational pragmatism.

The impulse to reject the harsh truth is the reason Israeli leaders and politicians do not dare to bring the truth to the people. The statesmen include not only those from the moderate and dovish factions, but also those who are skeptical of the peace process. Instead, they declare, "we should compromise with the Arabs in return for peace or at least for non-belligerancy." But if such a peace is unobtainable on any account — then these declarations endanger our people.

Declarations by our leaders about our readiness for partial withdrawal from the occupied territories in return for a peace settlement serve only as tranquilizers. They prevent Israel from taking adequate measures to secure her very existence while there is still time.

The arguments of those Israelis who contend that it is possible to reach a settlement with the Arabs in return for compromises can be divided into three groups:

A. The Rationalistic Argument:

"We recognize the fact," say the proponents of this argument, "that the Arabs would like to expel us from our land. But the Arabs know that they will not succeed in doing this. As befits Oriental merchants, they put forward maximum demands and claims. However, in fact, they would be prepared to accept less than our total expulsion and would agree to peace at a suitable price."

B. The Idealistic Argument:

This argument is an emotional one and is based on "faith." This group believes that one can indeed discern a certain change of attitude among the more advanced and moderate Arabs. "These Arab circles," they say, "have accepted the existence of Israel as a fact and only seek a *modus vivendi* with us." This Israeli group urges us to be "flexible," so that we can strengthen these moderate Arab elements. Of course, for that we must be prepared to make far-reaching concessions.

C. The Military Argument:

"If we are strong," they say, "we shall be able to halt or prevent any Arab attack on us. We shall finally force them to accept our existence. At the same time, we must reduce, as much as possible, the Arab motivation to wage war against us. This can be done by voluntary withdrawal from most of the territories."

Let us examine these arguments:

Argument A. The Rationalistic Argument is prevalent among wide circles of all strata of Israeli society. Those who assert that one can talk reason with the Arabs ignore the fact that even before the Balfour Declaration in 1917, the Arabs steadfastly opposed Zionism and the establishment of a Jewish Homeland in Palestine. They sidestep the fact that the Arabs did not once even offer to accept any type of compromise. The Arabs never agreed to the Partition Plan proposed by the British Peel Commission in 1936. They never responded to the suggestion to establish a bi-national state when it was advanced by the Israel radical-left party, Mapam. They strenuously opposed the U.N. resolution calling for the partition of the country between us and the Arab states. They still oppose the State of Israel. During all these years, it was not the Arabs who behaved like haggling Oriental merchants. The Israelis were those who acted like petty shop dealers and never stopped offering new proposals. We tried to sell them our know-how in technology, science, industry and agriculture. We offered them cultural ties and friendship. We suggested financial aid. Frequently, our leaders secretly met with "moderate" Arab statesmen. All these endeavors failed. They led to the same answer: "We don't want your help. Get out of Palestine which is our country."

Argument B. The Idealistic Argument is prevalent among Israeli leftist and progressive circles. Among them are those who are convinced that there are moderate Arabs, ready to come to terms with Israel under certain painful conditions, of course. But this argument does not stand up to the test. In the course of 60 years, it is impossible to find one Arab leader or one group which is ready to declare it will recognize the State of Israel or the right of Jews to the Land of Israel.

Not a single Arab writer or intellectual has yet published a proposal for a solution. The only document that they produced was the "Palestinian Covenant" which declared the sole rights of the "Palestinian people" to all the areas of Palestine. This Covenant, signed without exception by all Arab leaders, states that there is no place in the area for Israel, or for the Israelis.

In spite of all these facts, the dovish-progressive circles continue to believe that if not today then perhaps tomorrow, Israel shall succeed in bringing about a change in this attitude.

Let us take up this argument. Assume that there is a chance for a change in the Arab attitude, an argument, incidentally, close to the rationalistic mentality of Westerners. We take this chance in view of the fact that Arab nationalism, like Zionist nationalism, is nurtured by a respective historical past. Just as we strove for generations for the renewed independence of Israel, and the return to Zion, so do the Arabs aspire today for a revival of Pan-Arab and Pan-Islamic splendor.

In the time of the Caliphs, an Arab Empire stretched from Morocco and the south of Spain in the West — to Afghanistan in the East. This Islamic Empire constituted not only a great military power, but also the single cultural wing of light during the darkness of the Middle Ages.

Modern educated Arabs remember their days of glory. But they also have not forgotten Turkish rule which lasted for centuries, nor the humiliation they suffered under European colonial power. At present, they believe the time has come to renew the Arab hegemony in the Middle East and become a world power again. Only Israel stands in the way to realize this Arab ambition.

The territory of Israel is the most important link in the Pan-Arab continuity. As in ancient times, it constitutes a bridge between Asia, Africa and Europe. The State of Israel separates the Arab countries of North Africa from the Arabic and Islamic countries of Asia. Frequently, the Arabs have declared that Israel is a cancer in their body. There can not be peace with Israel, they say, as long as there is no territorial continuity between all the Arab lands. Thus, the Arabs never gave up, of their own free will, their claims to the territory of Israel which comprises the link joining together the countries of the Arab world.

Under Turkish rule, the Arabs sunk into a scientific and technological regression. The very existence of the modern State of Israel increases their frustration. It is obvious to them that as long as we are here, they will be unable to assume a dominant role in the area.

The nationalistic motivation of the Arabs derives also from the traditions of heroism of Saladin's crushing victories over the Crusaders and his destruction of the "Kingdom of Jerusalem," which had existed in the Holy Land for over a hundred years.

The Arabs are convinced that history will repeat itself and that just as the Crusader Kingdom fell under the sword of Saladin and ended with the expulsion of the Christians, so, too, will the Jewish State become an historical episode.

It should be remembered that while the Jews, who are zealous and impatient people, constantly suggest compromise and solutions, the Arabs patiently prepare for the propitious moment to act.

Argument C. The Military Argument says that Israel can make an agreement with the Arab states from a position of strength. This is one point all Israeli governments have stressed. But this premise does not stand up to the test.

We can only assume that if Israel will possess military superiority over the Arabs, the latter will be convinced that there is no chance to defeat us, or at least to achieve some political or territorial gain. Only then is there a probability that Israel will not be attacked.

But can Israel maintain such superiority for long?

Both Israeli and foreign diplomats as well as military men maintain that Israel is the dominant power in the Middle East. It can hold back any combination of Arab armies. But they also warn that this advantage will not last very long.

Following the Yom Kippur War and the oil embargo, the Arabs vaulted into an unprecedented position of wealth. Now they are able to acquire vast amounts of armaments. They are building a powerful military machine which they will use not to make compromises, but to destroy Israel.

The Defense Minister of the former Labor Government of Israel said that in ten years, arms will be so expensive that it will be impossible to settle the Arab-Israel conflict by means of war. His statement is only partially correct. While arms may become too expensive *for us*, the Arabs will have the financial resources to buy them. Considering our present economic situation, we cannot even afford to buy the arms that are needed to maintain the balance of power in the Middle East. Since the Arab wealth in petro-dollars is growing by the hour, Israel is bound to lose the arms race.

The Jewish population in Israel is three million, compared to a vast human reservoir of one hundred million Arabs. Egypt alone contains 40 million persons.

Soon, the Arabs will be able to mobilize an army of millions against Israel. They will be armed with the most sophisticated weapons.

How many defenders can Israel mobilize? It is, after all, a small nation with limited financial resources and population. Without destroying Israel's economic base, how many men can it pull away from the production lines?

True, Israel possesses a qualitative and technological superiority. But the "quality gap" between us and the Arabs constantly is diminishing. The day will come, and it may be sooner than we think, when Israel will be unable to resist an Arab attack.

Will nuclear weapons save Israel?

Many Israelis who are apprehensive of our future, see nuclear weapons as a last resort to deter the enemy.

Foreign sources report that Israel is in possession of ten to twenty atomic bombs. I do not know if this is true. But even if it were 50, we must take for granted that if the Arabs do not have the atomic bomb yet, they will aquire it in the near future. With so much money at their disposal, the Arabs will have no difficulty to induce scientists and engineers to build nuclear weapons for them

Israel must consider the fact that 80 per cent of the Israeli (Jewish) population is concentrated in a relatively small area. Assuming that the enemy drops a few atom bombs on this area, almost all of Israel will be wiped out.

On the other hand, the hundred million Arabs are spread over millions of square miles on two continents.

We might manage to retaliate in time and drop our bombs on their territory. Their casualties would be heavy, indeed, but all the twenty Arab states would survive. Not so Israel, which would no longer exist. Should Israel drop the first bomb, the Arabs will always have the opportunity to retaliate and the result will be exactly as outlined above.

The inference of this reasoning is that Israel can not rely on nuclear weapons for her security.

We must not overlook another aspect of the problem.

A few months before the Camp David agreement the President of Egypt declared that he is prepared to sacrifice a million Egyptians "to liberate Palestine." President Sadat is a man of his word. And despite his recent "peace offensive," his pronouncement should be taken seriously. In renewed aggression against Israel, Egypt, without doubt, will join, and even lead, Arab forces.

13. A QUESTION OF SURVIVAL

The gloomy conclusions of the previous chapter do not leave us any hope for a peaceful settlement of the conflict. All the liberals who believe in compromise and all those who think that we must find an understanding even with our enemies, will be disappointed.

I wish to stress again that my conclusions are neither hawkish nor belligerent. They are the result of the analysis of the existing situation in the Middle East. I stress this point in order to clear away the illusion which many people harbor that "things will somehow turn out for the best" and thus the Jewish people will avert another disaster.

Most people live in inertia. They do not perceive that one day a drastic change for the worse might occur. People find it difficult to visualize a calamity or sudden death which might strike them or their country. This is a psychological fact which in part explains the behavior of the Jews in the Holocaust. They optimistically went to work in the "Labor Camps," although they were warned by the few eyewitnesses who escaped. They simply did not believe them.

People only awake to action when calamity strikes. They fought back in the Warsaw Ghetto. But then it was too late.

The State of Israel, which paid the price of five wars to win Zion restored, will not give up its independence without a struggle. Israel will have to take adequate measures to face the Arab threat.

The Arab states are supplied by the U.S. and the European

countries with vast amounts of war material. The Arabs pay for these weapons with petro-dollars they exhort from the same countries who supply them with arms.

Most of these Western states proclaim their friendship towards Israel and concern for its well-being.

When Israel objects that the supply of arms to its enemies and the assertion of friendship to Israel are contradictory, the U.S. and the Europeans reply: "We also supply arms to Israel and thus keep the balance between the two sides."

But this reply is far from convincing or even honest. The Americans and the Europeans realize quite well — as we do — that Israel can not compete for long in this arms race. But even if we would achieve this balance of power, I would say:

We have no intention to die like the gladiators of old in the Middle East arena while the arms merchants look on with satisfaction from the heights of Capitol Hill and the Kremlin.

It is needless to say that any appeal to the conscience of nations and governments to stop the supply of war material to the enemies of Israel will be useless.

For the suppliers, vested interests, their economy, full employment in their arms factories will outweigh the destruction of the Jewish State.

For self-preservation, Israel must try to stop this flow of armament to the Arabs. It must prevent the Arab armies from achieving superiority over the Israel Defense Forces.

Discussing this matter with Israeli military experts, two lines of possible action are indicated.

A. A Blockade of Enemy Seaports and Lines of Supply.

Historically, a military blockade of this type is a legitimate action taken by the countries who are at war.

The Arab states are in a formal state of war with Israel. Therefore, it is our right to cut their supply lines. Of course, Israel does not have the military potential to blockade all enemy ports and airports. According to military experts, however, Israel does have adequate means to hit selective targets.

If Israel does attack various supply targets, it will come into direct conflict with the countries selling the weapons. We may assume that when Israel sinks some transport ships in enemy waters, or shoots down aircraft carrying spare parts to the Arabs, there will be an outcry against Israel among the nations shipping these arms.

But the citizens of those countries might pose a question to their own governments. Is it really necessary to endanger the lives of their young men in order to give in to Arab blackmail? Should governments be allowed to sacrifice young lives to enrich the powerful oil cartels and the big arms producers? Is bowing to the Arabs the only way to fuel the world's economy?

The pressures on Israel and the surrender to Arab blackmail is a new version of the policy of appeasement to Hitler and Nazi Germany which included the betrayal of Czechoslovakia. This appeasement policy led to World War II, the devastation of Europe, and the death of millions of people.

Today historians agree that a firm stand against Nazi blackmail would have prevented this disaster.

But evidently the politicians have learned nothing. Once more they display the same shortsightedness. They turn to "easy" temporary remedies; that is, pressure against Israel. Is there really no other solution of the West's oil problem?

The oil that the Western industrialized nations depend on comes mostly from desert areas inhabited by the Bedouin tribes of Saudi Arabia, Kuwait and Libya. The sheiks and "kings" of these tribes are members of OPEC, the oil producing cartels, which arbitrarily fix the price of oil. It is a well-known fact that these Bedouin are not the producers of the "black gold." They do not possess the technological knowledge, nor sophisticated equipment needed for these operations. These, plus the luxuries of the Western Civilization, are being supplied by the U.S. and other Western countries.

In these circumstances, one must wonder why the Western nations are yielding to the Arab threats of an oil embargo. Why do they consent to pay such exorbitant prices for that oil, prices that endanger the economic structure of the West.

Undoubtedly the Western nations could base their dealings with OPEC on a purely commercial basis, and once and for all, exclude the Arab-Israel political issue from the oil business.

Such a step would not only put an end to the blackmailing tactics of the Arabs, it would also lead to an economic recovery and renewed prosperity of the Western world without resorting to the export of war material to the enemies of Israel.

I do not delude myself that such rational arguments or even public opinion, for that matter, will in any way change the pro-Arab opinions of Western politicians. Their reaction to an Israeli blockade would probably be increased pressure, threats and perhaps even sanctions.

But Israel could also retaliate if it would be pushed against the wall. Israel could even use the same weapon that the Arabs are employing against Israel: the oil weapon.

The Arab threat to close the oil tap is also at the disposal of Israel.

Most oil fields in Saudi Arabia, the Persian Gulf, Egypt and Libya are in a range of only one thousand miles of Israel. (See Map)

After the "Entebbe Operation," which was 2,200 miles away, any possibility of an Israeli strike should be taken seriously.

B. The Alternative of a Preventive War.

The advantage of launching a preventive war against the Arab confrontation states is often discussed by the Israeli public.

Considering that we live in an atmosphere of terrorism and war, it is obvious that the solution of "let's finish with the Arabs once and for all and have peace," should be suggested.

In the Yom Kippur War, even though Israel was taken by surprise, it defeated the Arab armies on two fronts in only sixteen days, and with relatively small losses.

According to military experts throughout the world, the Israel Defense Forces still has great superiority over the Arab armies, despite their constant arming. The thinking is that it would be reasonable to destroy the Arab forces before they achieve the superiority that will enable them to fulfill their aspirations: the destruction of Israel.

Most Israelis are convinced that while a preventive strike might be successful militarily, it would not achieve the proper solution. Their objections are:

a. "Let us assume we already have destroyed the Arab armies and have occupied Cairo and Damascus. The superpowers will not tolerate this victory. They will force us to evacuate these "new occupied territories." Soon, the Arab states will rebuild their war machines as they have done in the past. We shall again face the same fully-armed enemy. So what have we gained?

b. "The United States will impose sanctions on Israel. The U.S. will stop the supply of arms and also cut off financial aid. How shall we fight or sustain ourselves without American aid?"

c. "The Soviet Union will not tolerate the collapse of her Arab client states. They serve as bases for her interests in the Middle East and Africa. The U.S.S.R. will send military forces against Israel."

Let us examine these objections.

If the supported American sanctions mean halt in the supply of military equipment and financial aid, then obviously the sting of such sanctions will be neutralized by the very fact of the Israeli victory.

While we would not remain in Egypt and Syria, we would disarm their armies and prevent their rearming for many years, as did the Allies in Germany after World War II. As a result of this preventive action, Israel will finally be rid of the threat to her existence. It will be able to reduce its armed forces; shorten the duration of military service; and cut the military budget.

Each year, thousands of young Israelis would be transferred from Army service to production lines. Israel would enter a period of economic growth and prosperity that will enable her to withstand any sanctions.

In conclusion, only a superior military power can induce Israel to abandon her positions. But it should be quite clear that Israel will not be intimidated by a show of force. In order to subdue Israel, a very large expeditionary force is required. But then Israel will not surrender as did Czechoslovakia in 1939. Israel would fight for her survival as did Finland or North Vietnam, two nations who battled like heroes against the superpowers.

Since the establishment of the State of Israel in 1948, not one day has elapsed without threats and pressures being directed at Israel whether by the U.S. or the Soviet Union — and sometimes, by both at the same time. Yet, throughout this whole period, the superpowers refrained from any military action against Israel.

Indeed, why should the U.S. or Russia sacrifice its sons?

What vital interests do they give up because of Israeli dominance in the Middle East?

Does the West fear another oil embargo by the Arabs? The mere presence of a strong Israel in the area will certainly prevent it. The assertion in the West that the Arabs must be supported and armed to prevent a Russian take-over of the oilfields of the Persian Gulf is an absurdity. How can the Arabs who were defeated by the Israeli Army stand up against a superpower? And is it conceivable that a country like the Soviet Union would cut off the life-line of the West and bring retaliation or cause a World War?

The U.S. and the U.S.S.R. often have conflicting interests around the globe, including the Middle East.

Each side tries to outmaneuver its opponent by using gifts one day, and threats the next.

We must keep in perspective the fact that the Middle East — and even oil — are not of utmost importance to the U.S. and the Soviet Union. It is doubtful whether any rational government would sacrifice thousands of its sons to achieve an insignificant advantage for its security.

Often, statesmen and the media warn that the Middle East constitutes a "powder-keg" which endangers world peace. At the same time they insinuate that Israel is a "fuse" which should be removed.

These warnings are not valid.

Why should a local war in the Middle East be more dangerous to the world than a war in Africa or the Far East?

Should a World War break out, Israel will not be the cause. The crucial issues are between the superpowers. Only they are responsible for a conflagration.

The warnings sent to Israel are no more than a form of psychological warfare, attempting to induce the Jewish State to give up some of its territory.

Once Great Britain and France interfered with the affairs of the Middle East. Today it is the U.S. and the Soviet Union. Peace in the area would have been achieved long ago and a modus vivendi between the Arabs and Israel would have been arrived at if all these powers would have kept their "diplomatic hands" off this region.

14. THE TERRITORIAL IMPERATIVE

When the founders of the Zionist movement came to the Promised Land at the end of the Nineteenth Century, they found a desolate, almost empty country. It was a land which could absorb millions of immigrants. They were convinced that the few Arab inhabitants of Palestine would welcome the Jews, who were their Semitic cousins and who would bring prosperity to the country.

The Jewish leaders, founders of the Zionist organization, formulated the Zionist ideology in the liberal, equalitarian spirit of the Nineteenth Century. They sincerely believed that Jews and Arabs would live side by side in Palestine, without a need to dispossess a single Arab farmer of his land. but at the same time, they took it for granted from the very beginning that the Jewish population would in time turn into a decisive majority and that eventually a Jewish sovereign state would be established.

This ideology was accepted as valid by all Zionist leaders, including the liberal, Dr. Chaim Weizmann; the nationalist, Ze'ev Jabotinsky; and the socialist, David Ben-Gurion. The unshakable belief in the just actions of the Zionist ideology led the Zionists to repeated efforts to reach a settlement and understanding with the Arab neighbors. These efforts continue to this very day.

The founders of Zionism could not foresee the great advance which would take place in the Twentieth Century in medical sciences, including discovery of penicillin, sulfa, Salk vaccines, etc. They could not anticipate that the Arab population of Palestine — riddled with disease and high infant mortality — would emerge in a few decades with one of the highest birthrates in the world: four per cent, doubling each twenty years. Furthermore, the Jewish leaders also had no idea that this backward and fatalistic Arab population would become extremely militant, a fact that we are witnessing today.

The conditions that existed during the First Zionist Congress have changed completely.

The present leaders of Israel, in whose hands lie the nation's life and future, should re-evaluate the new position of Israel, without any illusions or preconceived ideas. They ought to free themselves of the doctrine that Arabs and Jews will be able to live peacefully in Israel.

According to our Demographic Tables in Chapter 5, the Arab population of Israel will reach a majority in both "Greater Israel" comprising the "occupied territories" and in the limited border area of pre-1967. The only difference is that one will occur 60 years earlier.

Some might raise the question, "What is wrong with a secular state as proposed by the Palestinians, a state in which the Jews will be a minority?"

This proposition is an absurdity. The fundamental idea of the Zionist movement was to gather persecuted Jews dispersed among the nations and bring them back to the ancient homeland where they would be a majority and masters of their own destiny in their own sovereign state. If our fate should be to become a minority under the Arabs, the Jews would have preferred to remain within the "fleshpots" of the Western countries.

If we are determined that Israel should not come to an end in a hundred years and if we want our children and grandchildren to live in an independent Jewish State, then only two alternatives are at our disposal:

a. Disregarding their numbers, we can deny the Arabs of Israel parliamentary voting rights. We can keep them suppressed, in a condition similar to South Africa. But this solution is a contradiction to our way of life.

b. As was done after World War II in Poland, Russia, East Germany and other places in the world, we can transfer the Arab population.

Regarding the "legitimate rights of the Palestinians":

The Jewish people does not recognize anyone's rights to the land that bears the Biblical name of our nation: The Land of Israel. Our right to the land of our ancestors is an undisputable

65

fact. Moreover, our ancient homeland today is again under Jewish rule. Legalistic arguments will certainly not induce us to give up parts of our country.

But it is not only that the so-called Palestinians do not have any political rights over the Land of Israel, they do not have any rights over the very soil on which they reside. In the past, these lands belonged to Jewish farmers. Jewish farmers did not sell their lands. The Arab *fellahin* live, as a matter of fact, on absentee Israeli property, even though it must be admitted that they do so in good faith. But from the moment the legal owners return and claim ownership, the lands should be handed over to the Jewish people.

This is similar to the story told of the soldier who went off to war, but did not return. Years went by. The man was declared dead. The widow remarried. She had children with a second husband. And then, one day, the missing soldier reappeared, being discovered in a forgotten prisoners' camp. Obviously, this was a personal tragedy to both sides. However, the soldier's property, his house, his farm, must be reinstated. He is the lawful owner.

This can be accomplished on a humane basis, over a period of one or two generations, including agrarian reform, or by compensation.

We have been dealing with two dangers to the existence of Israel: the danger of being annihilated by superior Arab armies and the danger to Jewish supremacy in Israel by the tremendous Arab birthrate. We also pointed out possible ways to overcome both these dangers.

But there is a third danger, no less serious than the two others, and that is, our own Jewish natural increase.

Let us consider again the demography of Israel, illustrated on the graph in this chapter.

Curve A indicates the growth of the Jewish population without any significant immigration.

Curve C shows the increase of the Arab population in "Greater Israel."

The intersection of both curves in 1 is the lowest limit of Arab Jewish parity, i.e. 30 years. At that time, the Jews and Arabs will each number five million.

Curve B shows the Jewish population, assuming an optimal

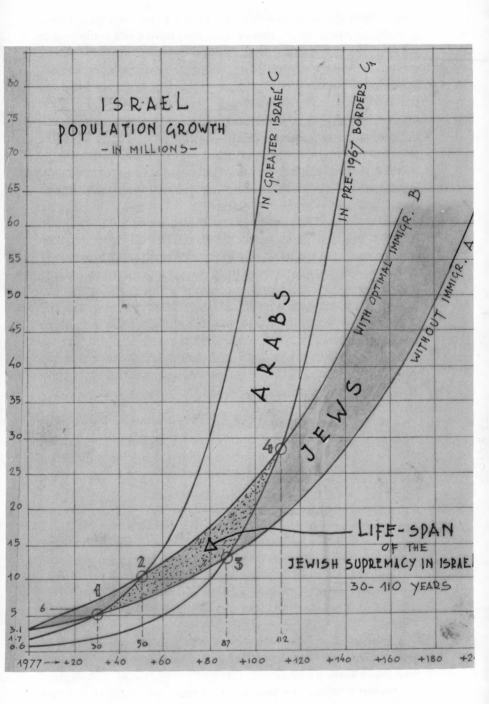

immigration. The intersection of this curve with the same curve C at point 2 will occur in about 50 years. The Jews and Arabs will number at that time over 10 million each, a total of over 20 million.

Curve C indicates the growth of the Arab population in the pre-1967 area; the intersection of this curve with Curve A at point 3 in 85 years, shows that the Jews and Arabs will number 13.5 million each in the "small" Israel.

The upper limit of parity will occur in about 110 years, at point 4. At that time, Jews and Arabs each will number 27 million — a total of 55 million, inhabiting the miniscule area of 8,000 sq. miles of the pre-1967 Israel.

The rhomboidal area 1, 2, 3, 4, represents the "life span" (30-110) years of the State of Israel.

If we contemplate again Curve A, we realize that in 200 years, the number of Jews in Israel may come out to about 65 million. This will be from natural increase only — without any significant immigration.

To most people, 200 years away is shrouded in the fog of the future.

But the U.S. recently celebrated its bicentennial. In the eyes of the average American the days of George Washington do not seem especially far away. That era is considered modern history.

For Israelis it seems only yesterday that Dr. Theodor Herzl inaugurated the First Zionist Congress in Basel, and that was nearly 100 years ago.

Let us also remember the fact that when the U.S. declared her independence, her population was 1,950,000; less than there are in Israel at present. But in 200 years, the U.S. grew into a nation of more than 200 million inhabitants.

Of course, the U.S. could absorb this rapid increase because it offered vast fertile lands, natural resources and, after the Revolutionary War and the War of 1812, no serious enemies.

Israel's crucial problem is what is termed "territorial imperative," or: adequate territory for the development of Israel.

The area of "Greater Israel" today, including the West Bank, the Gaza Strip, and the Golan Heights does not exceed 12,000 square miles. About 60 per cent of it is arid land. Can 70 million people subsist on an area that size?

We are not, of course, taking into account a large Arab population. Our assumption is that, if in a few decades the Arab population in Israel will be large, the Jewish State will have ceased to exist. We assume a Jewish majority of at least 85 per cent.

To illustrate what the future Jewish population might be like in 200 years, let us assume that one-third of the population of the U.S., about 70 million, is squeezed into a state, the size of New Jersey. Even in the most populated areas of the world, there is no comparable density. Modern biology states that each species must have a certain, fixed territory in order to exist.

In such a congested area, people are bound to suffer from pollution. And as has been demonstrated in famous biological experiments with rats that were allowed to multiply in a limited area, they may even go out of their minds.

The following objections may arise:

"Why should we care for future generations? Let them solve their own problems." Or: "The forecast of a population explosion is a matter that concerns the whole world; what may happen to other people may also be our fate."

The reply to this objection is:

a. Israel must become a larger nation. If in the future Israel will not reach tens of millions, it will not be able to hold out militarily against the hundreds of millions of Arabs who will then surround it, and it will not be able to sustain itself economically and culturally, and become a modern, developed country.

b. Scientists predict that in the future, nations will struggle over living space. Only those with agricultural land reserves will be able to survive. Israel must look after itself, as do other nations.

c. The civilized nations of the West have reached a certain numerical balance. Over the generations, Jews lost the elite of its people in persecutions, pogroms, holocausts and assimilation. Now we must make up for these losses and reach a balance as do other developed nations.

How should Israel treat the problem of the Jewish overpopulation? Should she limit her future population to ten million or twenty million?

Such planning would involve birth control and the curbing of Jewish immigration. That means a Jewish, anti-Zionist

"White Paper." Not only does this contradict the fundamentals of Zionist ideology, it also is impossible to implement, as the large religious sector in Israel is against birth control. In view of the foregoing analysis, we must say that the cession of territory in the Sinai which was the only land reserve for future Israeli farmers was, to say the least, a big mistake.

This Israeli mistake has been quickly seized upon by Egypt which is now completing tunnels under the Suez Canal and water pipelines from the Nile, with the intention to settle one million Egyptian *fellahin* in the Sinai.

Israel must already begin looking now for additional territories to secure her future development.

In the middle of World War I, in 1916, France and Britain signed a pact named after the two diplomats who signed it: the Sykes-Picot agreement. The two colonial powers divided the Syrian Province of the Ottoman Empire among themselves. They divided the spoils even before the territory fell into their hands. Looking at the Map of the Middle East, we find that those Syrian and Arab deserts bordering on present-day Syria, Jordan and Saudi Arabia are divided by straight lines. In accordance with the Sykes-Picot Pact, this division was made after World War I into a French zone of influence (Syria and Lebanon) and an English zone (present Iraq, Israel and Jordan). Such straight lines nearly always indicate an arbitrary division, without any ethnic consideration.

A desert is similar to a sea. It is actually a no-man's land. The desert, like the sea, separates the bordering countries. It has, however, important geopolitical and military aspects.

The Syrian and Arab deserts were divided by colonial powers, long before a new factor in the area — the State of Israel — was established.

While colonial rule has long since ceased to exist, Israel has become the dominant power in the Middle East.

In this new situation, Israel must demand re-partition of these deserts which are essential to her security.

Thanks to Israeli technology and efforts, these arid areas in the future will turn into fertile lands and will serve as the agricultural reserve for the developing Israel.

The Arabs possess a land reserve of nearly five million square miles, as against the 12,000 square miles for Israel which includes the "occupied territories." Their lives and their future are in no way endangered. The Arabs should realize, therefore, that there can not be peace in the Middle East unless Israel has the same chance for development and survival.

Another aspect of the situation is:

The fact that the Jews in Israel will multiply and become numerous, even without any immigration. This comes as a shock to most Jews and shatters their fundamental concept of "aliya"; Jewish immigration. They considered aliya to be the core of Zionist ideology and absolutely vital to the future of Israel.

For whereas the Jews in Israel will multiply and become a great nation, the number of Jews in the Diaspora will constantly diminish due to assimilation. In a few generations, only insignificant Jewish communities will survive outside of Israel.

The inference here is that in the future, a Jewish people will exist only in Israel. Another indication is that if Israel should be destroyed by the Arab states, the Jews of Israel will disperse again and the Jewish people will cease to exist anywhere in the world.

The State of Israel is most interested in aliya — Jewish immigration — cited in the Israeli Constitution. All Israelis want their coreligionists to return to the Land of their ancestors. They deplore the constant loss of Jewish genius to other ethnic groups. But the Jews in the Diaspora (the area outside of Israel) as well as in Israel should realize that today the aliya is no longer indispensable for the future of the State of Israel.

There is an historical analogy to this: When the exiled Jews of Babylon were permitted to return to the Land of Israel (about 500 B.C.) by the Persian Emperor Cyrus, only about twenty thousand followed their leaders, Ezra and Nehemia. Three hundred and fifty years later, these Jews had become a nation of many millions, and were able — under the Maccabees — to defeat the powerful Greek armies. The Maccabees reinstated the Jewish sovereignty and founded the Hasmonean Dynasty which lasted until the Roman times.

The Jewish people of today are the direct descendants of that nation. The bulk of the Jews who remained in Babylon — like the ten tribes before — were lost to the Jewish people.

15. SECURE FRONTIERS

After the Six-Day War, when the Golan Heights and the West Bank came under Israeli control, it was felt that these areas were needed to ensure Israel's security.

In those days, Israeli military experts said that the Suez Canal is the best obstacle against an Egyptian invasion; that the Jordan River is the "natural border," between Israel and the Jordan; and that the Golan Heights will protect Israel from a Syrian attack in the north.

Six years later, the Yom Kippur War erupted and that great obstacle, the Suez Canal, did not stand up to the test. The Egyptians crossed the canal. In one night, they transported two armies to the Israeli side. The famous, fortified line, known as the "Bar-Lev Line," collapsed, although it should be pointed out that the line was undermanned because of the Yom Kippur holiday.

In history, fortified military lines do not hold out against surprise attacks. The French Maginot Line and the German Siegfried Line are perfect examples.

In addition to the heroism of the Israeli soldiers, what saved Israel on the Egyptian front was the vast desert of the Sinai. These areas enabled the Israeli Army to employ its superior maneuverability, and then stop the enemy, far away from the densely populated urban centers.

On the northern fronts, the undermanned Israeli lines did not hold out against the Syrian blitz for long, but long enough to enable the Israeli forces to reorganize for a counterattack. The Syrian forces swept over the Golan Heights. They soon reached the outskirts of Jewish settlements in the plains. The few Jewish kibbutzim on the Golan were evacuated. Only the vast unsettled areas which were far from the populated centers of the Golan, as in the Sinai, stopped the enemy and prevented a disaster. Of course, in the last analysis, it was the human factor that tipped the scales to Israel.

There was no invasion by the Jordanian army during the Yom Kippur War. But if King Hussein would have attacked us by surprise, then the Jordan River — which is just a narrow stream — would certainly not have served as an obstacle to Jordanian armed forces.

I am always amazed when I hear people say that the Jordan River is a "secure border." For centuries, armies have crossed wide rivers such as, the Rhine, the Elbe, the Oder, the Vistula, the Dniepper, and Danube, etc. and they have done so without sophisticated equipment.

There is a custom in Israel to take foreign visiting VIPs up to the Golan Heights. Here they see pre-1967 gun emplacements looking down on the settlements in the valley below. The visitors are indeed impressed and convinced that the Golan is essential to the security of Israel.

But we should ask ourselves: After the Golan Heights will be densely populated and covered not only by agricultural settlements but also by Jewish towns — what "line" will defend them? What will the future security border of the Golan be?

We also show visiting VIPs the "narrow waist of Israel": the nine miles that separate the old border of the West Bank from the Mediterranean. Here, too, the visitors are impressed and agree that if Israel gives up land it can be easily cut in two. They understand the Israeli argument that Judea and Samaria are the hinterland needed for the security of Israel.

And again we must ask: What will happen when Judea and Samaria become densely populated with Jewish cities and villages? Will not these cities and villages be within the shooting range of artillery guns placed on the slopes of the Gilead mountains across the Jordan Valley? Is the Jordan Valley any wider than the "narrow waist of Israel"?

The average distance between the Jordan River and the Mediterranean Sea — between the ports of Haifa and Ashdod — is only 45 miles. More than 80 per cent of the Jewish population is concentrated in this trapeze-like area, which includes also the West Bank. This area comprises all the important cities of Israel, including Jerusalem and Tel Aviv and most of the industrial plants, the trade centers, the seaports and airfields.

In the Yom Kippur War Israel was attacked on two fronts. A unified military command is being organized by the Arab confrontation states with Israel. In this command, the central Jordanian sector will contain a force that in a surprise attack will overrun the 45 mile-wide central area of Israel and reach Tel Aviv and Haifa in a few hours.

Therefore, we can not accept the idea that the Jordan is an "ideal border" which will protect the eastern flank of Israel.

In all the Arab-Israel wars after the War of Independence, the battles were fought far from the populated centers. Not one enemy aircraft managed to penetrate our skies, and not one bomb was dropped on our cities and towns.

The families prayed for the safety of their sons or husbands who were at the front. But at home, life went on. Morale was high. The theatres and cinemas were open. The latest news was discussed in the cafes.

The security of Israel was guarded by the fact that battles were fought in distant frontiers.

With future powerful Arab armies and the participation of Jordan, the present frontiers of Israel will no longer suffice to guarantee her security.

Only control by Israel over vast areas of the Syrian and Arabic deserts in the north, and the Sinai Desert in the south, will enable the Israel Defense Forces to contain invading Arab armies and provide security for Israel and her population.

Regarding secure borders, some assert that the modern, sophisticated electronic weapons and devices eliminate the need for wide defensive areas. With these instruments, they say, even a small country will be able to defend itself successfully.

Such assertions seem to me quite unreasonable. On the contrary, a small, densely-populated area is more vulnerable to long-range missiles and nuclear bombs than to conventional warfare.

One need not be a military expert to see that the chance of survival favors a dispersed population.

16. ISRAEL DOMINATES THE MIDDLE EAST

The world sees the conflict in the Middle East as a struggle between the Arabs and Israel over the ownership of the Land of Israel.

Actually, that definition is misleading. The reality is that it is only an Arab problem. It is they who want the Land which is in Israel's possession and which can be taken away only by war.

Most nations believe that if only a compromise could be reached between the two contestants, peace would arrive. They feel that with one stroke the Arab threat of an oil embargo would disappear. Oil prices would drop. The Western nations would again enjoy economic recovery and prosperity.

But the truth is that the Arab economic confrontation with the West would take place even if Israel did not exist. The real danger is the challenge of the Arab-Islamic world to Western civilization. This battle is still in its infancy. Its meaning has not yet penetrated the consciousness of the West, despite the Islamic revolution of Khomeini in Iran.

It does not mean that the Arab-Israel conflict is a marginal issue. On the contrary, Israel is the first target in the challenge. Israel lies in the center of the Arab world, "a thorn in the Arab flesh." Therefore, Israel must be eliminated at all cost. The very existence of a Jewish State is an obstacle to Arab hegemony in the Middle East. At the same time, this conflict is a useful instrument to the fulfillment of Arab global aspirations.

The national desires of the Arabs today is to restore the glory and power they had in the era of the Caliphs when Islam reigned over a vast Empire stretching from Morocco on the Atlantic Ocean to India in the east.

In the Middle Ages, the Arabs were the foremost World Power. For centuries, the Moors were masters of Spain and southern France. The Islamic influence extended in modern times to the last century when Moslem Turks ruled over Greece and parts of Rumania. In the first decade of this century, they still held Bulgaria and Albania.

The dominant status of the Arabs changed following the discovery of America and the technological and industrial revolution in Europe. Their superiority gradually deteriorated until they were captured by colonial and imperialistic rulers. After World War II, colonial raids came to an end, and the Arab people began to dream of restoring their old glory.

The growing dependence of the industrialized Western countries on Arab oil gave the Arabs at least the means to pursue their ambition to again become a world power.

In his book *Policy of Defeat,* Joseph Chorba, former U.S. Air Force Intelligence Officer for the Middle East writes:

"Pierre Rinfret, a respected international economic advisor, informs us that humanity faces a worldwide depression because the oil-rich Arab countries are determined to destroy Israel and will bleed the energy-starved Western world unless better leadership is known."

Today, we see that his prediction is coming true.

The idea of using the oil embargo as a political weapon and raising the price for oil fourfold in one simple action was actually not an Arab brainstorm. It was inspired by their American partners, the oil companies; especially those operating in Saudi Arabia. These oil-producing cartels exploit the Arab-Israel conflict as a pretext for unprecedented money-making operations.

The greed of the American cartels is detrimental not only to the interest of their own country and to the security of Israel, but also to the economy of the Western world.

Mr. Chorba writes:

"As a matter of record in Congressional testimony, these multinational oil corporations were the executors of the direct orders of the Saudi Government for the Oil Embargo of 1973-74 against the industrial democracies thus undermining the United States strategic interest in the economic vitality of the Western Alliance. Even shipments to the United States Navy were not excluded from this embargo."

The reaction of the Western nations today to the Arab challenge may be compared to the state of affairs in the Roman Empire before its breakdown. The pursuit of the life of opulence on one hand and moral apathy on the other, combined to cause Rome's fall at the hands of the Goths and Vandals.

Mr. Chorba expresses a similar viewpoint:

"To ignore the challenge of OPEC is to accept the gradual loss of independence and well-being. It is time for the American body politic to affirm once and for all that our government at least was not created to foster the further enrichment of the very few. Present OPEC oil policy and our politics of defeat in not confronting it will otherwise sap not so much the arteries of our industry as the blood vessels of our national body and our moral tissue.

"Under the impact of the Arab oil weapon, the unity of Europe is now in jeopardy and the very fabric of European society seriously threatened."

I cannot accept the idea that the U.S. and the other Western industrialized countries are powerless against the Arab oil embargo blackmail, in as much as the Arabs are unable to produce a single barrel of oil without the aid of the West.

We must assume, therefore, that the Western countries are unwilling to stand up to the powerful oil companies and the producers of tanks, airplanes, missiles — all suppliers of the Arabs. Or perhaps they refrain from reacting forcefully because they fear a confrontation with Soviet Russia.

Mr. Chorba and other American experts urge the Western nations to act forcefully against the oil cartels and not give in to Arab blackmail. Also, they believe that a strong Israel will be a valuable ally to the West:

"But for the Arab conviction that fear of Soviet interposition nullifies the Western military option to seize the oil fields, would the oil cartel risk economic warfare with Western industrial society? This conviction is basically unfounded since a forthright and determined American policy will not be challenged militarily by the Soviet Union. The Kremlin has no national interest at stake in the affair, being basically self-sufficient in oil."

He continues:

"In the event of an oil consumer-producer confrontation forced upon the West by extortionist oil prices, the presence in the Middle East of a strong Israel could prove to be of great value."

We Israelis can only welcome these recommendations. But I doubt if they will fall on sensitive ears. The fact is that the United States will indeed apply pressure on Israel and not on the Arabs. The other Western nations will do the same.

It may be assumed that the West will probably not change its Arab policy. Israel alone will have to take care of herself.

The Jewish people made an essential contribution to Western culture. The ethical, moral and social values, the monotheistic religion, man's dignity and behavior — all these are of Hebrew origin. The great English historian, Arnold J. Toynbee, stated that Western civilization is based on two pillars: Judaism and Hellenism.

The Jews are part of the Western culture and civilization. It would be sad indeed if this civilization should come to an end at the hands of Islam.

But while the Western countries remain apathetic in the face of the Arab challenge, we Israelis can not afford to do so. Whereas the West, even under an Islamic civilization, might continue to exist, an Arab conquest of Israel today would mean the end of the Jewish people.

Israel will be obliged to take action against the Arab blackmail of the West. It would do this for its own sake, even against the wishes of the West.

The two superpowers, the Soviet Union and the U.S., are suspicious of one another. A look at the Map will show that a thousand-mile radius from Israel takes in a great part of southern Russia, including her rich oil regions of the Black and Caspian Seas. The presence of American bases in Israel would mean that jet bombers could fly over southern Russia and endanger her soft belly. No wonder the U.S.S.R. is so apprehensive of an American presence in the area.

What should our attitude be? Israel should consider that the thousand-mile radius extends both ways. In the case of a conflict between the powers, the presence of American bases in Israel would automatically cause Russian retaliation. Israel would be one of the first targets, suffering great losses and damage.

Should Israel really suffer these attacks because it is on the side of the West? Obviously not. In my opinion, our true interest lies in the U.S. withdrawal from the area in order to subdue Russian fears. At the same time, the Russians should withdraw from the Middle East to alleviate the fears of the West. Israel must not forget that Jews live not only in the West, but they also reside in the U.S.S.R., where there are about three million. I believe that a sound policy of Israel would be to reach a state of political non-alignment with the West, as well as with the East.

Military experts have pointed out that a single submarine could shut off the Hormuz Straits, connecting the Persian Gulf with the Indian Ocean (see Map), and thus virtually stop all Arab oil shipped to the West by tankers. There are, however, existing pipelines in the Syrian Desert. They connect the Arab oil wells from the Persian Gulf and the oil from Iraq with the Israeli port of Haifa on the Mediterranean Sea (see Map).

A strong Israel in control of these pipelines will guarantee the continuous flow of that precious commodity to the West, as well as to the East.

A strong dominant Israel in the area will, in all probability, constitute the stabilizing factor that will insure peace in the Middle East.